James MASON

SARAH THOMAS

BFI palgrave

A BFI book published by Palgrave

© Sarah Thomas 2018

All rights reserved. No reproduction, copy or transmission of this
publication may be made without written permission.

No portion of this publication may be reproduced, copied or transmitted
save with written permission or in accordance with the provisions of the
Copyright, Designs and Patents Act 1988, or under the terms of any licence
permitting limited copying issued by the Copyright Licensing Agency,
Saffron House, 6–10 Kirby Street, London EC1N 8TS.

Any person who does any unauthorized act in relation to this publication
may be liable to criminal prosecution and civil claims for damages.

The authors have asserted their rights to be identified as the authors of
this work in accordance with the Copyright, Designs and Patents Act 1988.

First published in 2018 by
PALGRAVE

on behalf of the

BRITISH FILM INSTITUTE
21 Stephen Street, London, W1T 1LN
www.bfi.org.uk

Palgrave in the UK is an imprint of Macmillan Publishers Limited,
registered in England, company number 785998, of 4 Crinan Street,
London, N1 9XW.

Palgrave® and Macmillan® are registered trademarks in the United States,
the United Kingdom, Europe and other countries.

ISBN: 978–1–84457–635–7 paperback

This book is printed on paper suitable for recycling and made from fully
managed and sustained forest sources. Logging, pulping and manufacturing
processes are expected to conform to the environmental regulations of the
country of origin.

A catalogue record for this book is available from the British Library.

A catalog record for this book is available from the Library of Congress.

(*previous page*) James Mason in *The London Nobody Knows* (1967)
Cover image: 'Odd Man Out' – James Mason 1947, Rex/Shutterstock.

CONTENTS

ACKNOWLEDGMENTS VI

1 INTRODUCTION 1
2 PERSONA 9
3 POWER 43
4 PERFORMANCE 83

NOTES 120
BIBLIOGRAPHY 125
FILMOGRAPHY 136
INDEX 141

ACKNOWLEDGMENTS

I would like to thank Martin Shingler, who has not only been an immensely supportive series editor, but also an important and encouraging figure throughout my career. Thanks also go to the staff at BFI Publishing and Palgrave Macmillan, especially Nicola Cattini and Sophia Contento. Thanks to the staff at the Margaret Herrick Library, the Warner Brothers Archive at USC and the BFI Library in the researching of this project, to Adrian Garvey and Paul Ward for the discussions, and to Oliver Carter for the hard-to-find films. I am indebted again to the wonderful Luella Forbes for her time, effort and company. Thanks to Lisa Richards, Steph Jones and Kate Egan for their valuable feedback and support. I am grateful to Adam Qureshi, who was there at the beginning of the project and continues to lend a thoughtful ear whenever needed. And special thanks to the excellent Mark McKenna, whose enthusiasm and care made writing this all the more fun.

1 INTRODUCTION

Halfway through Vivian Kubrick's behind-the-scenes documentary about her father's film *The Shining* (1980), James Mason appears. Dressed in a light grey Victorian suit and accompanied by a small group of friends and family, he introduces everyone to Jack Nicholson and Stanley Kubrick during a break in filming. His unexpected appearance can be explained – Kubrick was making the film at Elstree Studios where Mason was filming *Murder by Decree* (1979), and having worked together on *Lolita* (1962), Kubrick allowed the actor a rare guest pass to the set. Nevertheless, it is a deeply incongruous moment. We've just seen examples of Kubrick's meticulous staging, fractious relationship with Shelley Duvall, and Nicholson's energetic preparation for the scene where he breaks down the bathroom door with an axe (intercut with the completed scene), but suddenly this restrained, polite excitement descends onto the set. Mason's family are so very ordinary: aside from his wife, Clarissa, there are also two girls in their 'Sunday best' keen yet intimidated to meet Nicholson, and an elderly woman with an eminently recognisable 'grandmotherly' perm and thick glasses; yet everything about *The Shining* is so absolutely extraordinary, even behind the scenes. Mason stands in the middle, bisecting these spaces and people; not simply a combination of the ordinary and extraordinary, but also apart from both in his effortless smart appearance, calm aloofness, yet amiable, relaxed attitude.

But James Mason was an incongruous and contradictory figure; a star often positioned as one between worlds – between leading man and character actor, Hollywood and Britain, control and powerlessness, menace and allure, the ultimate Odd Man Out – and described by *Life* magazine as one whose 'sombre, sensual handsomeness arouses hopes and anxieties in women' (Osborne 1947: 33). Despite the randomness of using Vivian Kubrick's documentary as an opening to this book, what the short film reflects on around the production of *The Shining* parallels many of the subjects that I will explore around Mason's stardom, including this dissonance. The connection helps contextualise my study as an analytical history of Mason's career with its reference to *Lolita* and *Murder by Decree*, and where the figure of the American Kubrick (and his British-raised daughter) working amidst the British film industry hints at the attention paid to transnational statuses (and families) that will follow. Mason's cameo in the documentary comes immediately after Nicholson has defined himself as a 'celebrity' (and the endless, exhausting round of meeting so many people this role entails). At first it seems like Mason's own celebrity is being dismissed here – is he simply another person Nicholson-the-celebrity must meet? – but Vivian's commentary acknowledges the star and his visit as 'special'. The persistence of star persona (and the performance of self-as-image) runs throughout Nicholson's knowing presence – he is constantly playing up to Vivian's camera as 'Jack'. But equally, space is given over to discussions of the labour of acting and his own (and Duvall's) technical processes. Nicholson talks of his willingness to hand control over to someone else, and inherent in any discussion around Kubrick is the subject of power. There is even an (admittedly light-hearted) conversation about salaries when Danny Lloyd naively states that he 'must have $500 or $600!' by now. My analysis of James Mason mirrors these concerns, looking similarly at the screen and behind it over the course of its three chapters. It explores Mason's star labour and the issues of money and power that ran throughout his career and perceptions of its success. I will examine how he approached roles and developed performative technique, and I will consider different elements of Mason's star persona – from the image he played up to of 'the-man-you-love-to-hate' to his complex celebrity status, and even his 'ordinariness'.

The son of a textile merchant, James Mason was born in Huddersfield, Yorkshire, in 1909 and lived a comfortable life in the leafy part of the town's Croft House Lane. Before embarking on his acting career, he went to Marlborough College, read architecture at Cambridge University, and then on to London, Dublin and regional theatres before turning to the cinema. Between 1935 and 1943, he had minor roles in major British films, and major roles in minor films, building up a steady presence in the industry. His breakthrough was *The Man in Grey* (1943), and his star status was consolidated with the other Gainsborough Pictures melodramas that followed, where he was often cast as a menacing but romanticised anti-hero. The British public loved Mason and his brutal screen persona, voting him the most popular British star of 1946, by which time he had caught Hollywood's eye. He was just as rebellious off screen, constantly criticising the film industry and attempting to produce his own films. In disgust with the British film industry, he ran off to the United States in 1947, and then ran back in 1962 disgusted with Hollywood films. He married twice: first to Pamela Kellino in 1941 who went with him to Hollywood, where they had two children, Portland and Morgan. In 1964, they divorced acrimoniously with a financial settlement heavily in Pamela's favour. Compared to the turbulence of his first two decades of international stardom, the final twenty years of Mason's career seem low-key – in line with his reserved visit to *The Shining*'s set. After the divorce, he settled in Corsier-sur-Vevey, Switzerland, and from this base travelled extensively throughout Britain, Europe and the rest of the world to make films. In 1969, he met the Australian actress Clarissa Kaye whilst filming *Age of Consent* in Australia and they married two years later. He died in 1984. Throughout all this, he made over a hundred films with a handful usually cited as *really* significant, including *The Seventh Veil, Odd Man Out, The Reckless Moment, The Desert Fox, Julius Caesar, A Star Is Born, Bigger Than Life, North by Northwest, Lolita, Georgy Girl, Heaven Can Wait* and *The Shooting Party*.

Mason characterised his life and career as one of three ages: Britain and popular stardom (up to *Odd Man Out* [1947]), the Hollywood studio system (up to *North by Northwest* [1959]), and the British homecoming and movement into character roles (from *Lolita* to his death). This book too follows a 'three act structure', but takes a different path to Mason's view over its three chapters. Instead of exploring one period of Mason's life concurrently over each chapter, I wanted to analyse his stardom through modes of reading. I came to this project with a distinct interest in those conventional divisions – the movement between Hollywood and British cinemas, and the shift from leading man to character actor, bound together by a coherent star image of brooding exoticism/eroticism – but in the end, to simply concentrate on these boundaries did not sufficiently reflect the multiplicity (and at times shambolic nature) of Mason's career and persona. For example, many of his star-making roles of the mid-1940s could be categorised as supporting ones, he often occupied a secondary position in films focused on major female Hollywood stars, and he did not completely disappear from leading roles post-1962. My three chapters focus on methodological approaches to stardom: the star persona, economics and industry, and screen performance. Often in star studies these are explored concurrently, but what interested me was how separating them out articulated such a wide range of histories and versions of 'James Mason' beyond those already most established. I do not completely abandon chronology – the first two chapters use periodisation as a structuring technique to consider possible developments in image and labour – but I am wary of constructing more teleological readings where the problems of one era in turn create the features of another. One outcome of this is a repeated emphasis on Mason's post-1962 films – despite making up half of his filmic output, these are too often reduced to footnotes.

Chapter 2: 'Persona' begins by positioning Mason's star persona as illustrative of Richard Dyer's concept of structured polysemy, whereby multiple meanings converge and interact with each other to reinforce a coherent image or to contain oppositional elements where differences complicate but equally inform the wider persona (1998: 63–64). Dyer's description of images that may often 'be to some degree in opposition or contradiction' (ibid.: 64) rests on those contradictions being *available* so that they can be overtly held in tension, negotiated, or masked in the public sphere (through roles and promotional material) or the private/public sphere (circulated gossip). Across his whole career, Mason's public image was – at various times – made up of different aspects and identities, but most sustained attention has been paid to one particular element of his persona and how this predominantly contributes to scholarly readings or histories of British cinema. As well as providing an overview of his persona and responses to it, this chapter uses Mason to map developments in critical approaches to stardom: how an understanding of his persona illustrates the changing ways stars have been (and may be) analysed, and how modes of analyses feed back into definitions and interpretations of Mason's persona and the overall perception of his stardom. Aside from the inherent duality of the Mason image that dominates public discourse, what is also interesting within critical readings/retrospectives of the star is the degree to which some identities are absent or have only recently re-entered the discussion, especially those developed during his American career and beyond, which are centred around his ageing and his place within a quirky family setting and specific regional locale. Dyer comments that 'the possibilities of meaning are limited in part by what the text makes available' (ibid.: 64), and to some extent, I recognise that one of the 'texts' that produce star meaning must also include critical writing, be it scholarly or retrospective. Analyses and reflections on Mason's persona are part of the process whereby discourse 'masks' and/or 'reconciles' contradictory elements in their pursuit of a central subject of investigation that conventional biography, publicity and further primary sources may otherwise reveal.[1]

Chapter 3: 'Power' shifts focus away from reading Mason through the cultural meaning of his star image towards one that explores his professional labour status and career management through the question of 'power'. Starting with Mason's own commentary in his role as writer-documenter, I then place the star in the industries he worked in, using archival sources and industrial histories to draw together more information about his salaries, contracts, employment conditions and studio negotiations, talent agencies and his semi-freelance status. This contextualises and historicises Mason's account of his own power struggles within wider histories of professional labour and industrial structures. Mason – quite understandably – is concerned with his own failures in a singular sense; *he* made bad decisions, employers undervalued *him*, independent productions were centred around *his* star status and determination, and so on. But there is a need to step beyond a history and analysis of Mason *himself* to consider other histories of producers, stars and studios and how struggles around labour, power and independence form a bigger picture of film production in the twentieth century. This approach builds upon Paul McDonald's work, which called for a shift from the dominant mode of analysis of stars as 'fundamentally symbolic entities', recognising that whilst 'stars are texts, meaning, images and culture, they are also more than this [and it is] necessary to place stardom in a particular economic and industrial context' (2013: 3). New histories of labour organisation, professional agents and film production provide a bedrock to understanding some of Mason's own difficulties (and achievements) during his time in Hollywood and beyond, often revealing his experiences as much more conventional and shared than otherwise supposed. An analysis of the star through this methodological approach not only establishes further depth to his own star status, but contributes to industrial and economic analyses through a case study of an actor whose labour struggle is not an extreme of success *or* failure and one who moves between the UK, Hollywood and European production occupying contracted, semi-freelance and independent status.

Finally, Chapter 4: 'Performance' shifts attention back to Mason's screen work. His death in 1984 intensified evaluation of the star, especially his value as an actor, and, in addition to characterising him as the 'nearly man' of Hollywood stardom, many obituaries also emphasised his performative skills. Philip French in the *Observer* called him 'one of the four or five best film actors this country has produced' (1984: 19), and *The Evening Standard* described him as 'the actor who set a standard in excellence and maintained it' (Sheldon and Meilton 1984). The increased recognition of Mason's acting skills was apparent elsewhere. In a 1973 profile of the actor, the *New York Times* film critic Vincent Canby wrote that although

no longer the leading man he once was … for some time I've been thinking that Mason was becoming a better and more interesting actor with the passage of time, but having recently reseen *Lolita* and *North by Northwest* and *Georgy Girl*, it now occurs to me that he has always been superb.

Sidney Lumet, who directed Mason in four films (*The Deadly Affair* [1966], *The Sea Gull* [1968], *Child's Play* [1972] and *The Verdict* [1982]), commented that 'I always thought he was one of the best actors who ever lived. He always reminded me more of an actor in a theatre repertory ensemble than a movie star, and it was what made him so good' (qtd. in Morley 1989: 142–43). There is an obvious undercurrent of cultural judgment running through these reflections: Mason failed as a *star*, but – in the end – was victorious as an *actor*. The apparent conflict between the high and low cultural value of actor and star is, of course, limiting in scope, and scholarly analyses of stardom complicate this through their consideration of the performance of stardom on and off screen – of self/image and of character/role – and it is not what I am interested in here. Instead, I identify four thematic areas with which to analyse his performances: stage and screen, monologues and silences, tragedy and comedy, and intellectual distance and emotional empathy. This is partly to draw continuities across his career in terms of acting style and characteristics, and partly to expand analyses of Mason's screen work beyond those that neatly cohere with the dominant persona of the sardonic or romanticised perversity of his mid-1940s roles.

What remains is a star immensely difficult to pin down and in constant tension. Contradiction lies inherently within a star persona that has long been characterised through the transgressions of national context, romanticised violence, voice and look, and authority and rebelliousness. As I will examine, to this we can add excessive but reluctant narratives of celebrity and interplay between youth and ageing, national and regional. He pursued a career always in flux – running from one industry to another, between contracts and freelance status, and working extensively in transnational environments. And an acting style that negotiated registers, media form, genre and style to create sophisticated characterisation, and the performance of role and of self, is present throughout the whole of Mason's working life. Dissonant incongruity runs through James Mason's stardom, crossing boundaries of cultural image, labour status and acting technique, but in each sphere in markedly different ways.

2 PERSONA

'To be a successful film star as opposed to a successful film actor, you should settle for an image and polish it forever. I somehow could never quite bring myself to do that' (Mason qtd. in Hirschhorn 1977: 22). Thus James Mason sums up stardom and the management of his own public persona, identifying in it inconsistencies and idiosyncrasies. Typical of how critical studies conceptualise stars, Mason's star persona can be identified as multiple identities that lie between on-screen roles, promotional material and interviews, gossip, and the active role played by audiences, critics and the star himself in further articulating cultural meanings around that figure. These disparate meaning-making elements then cohere into a more singular public persona. In spite of Mason's above observation, wider discourse constructs a *very* polished and distinct meaning around the persona of 'James Mason', closely positioned through his star-making roles of the 1940s, irascible off-screen personality and career trajectory – from Britain to Hollywood and back again. This persona embodies a continual site of dualism and tension, usually fashioned as a form of romanticised aggression. Peter William Evans writes that 'the Mason persona exemplifies the conflict in men between competing instincts, a struggle reaching its most dramatic climaxes in his various encounters with women' (2001: 113). Andrew Spicer labels Mason 'the Byronic male' whose appeal lay in a combination of the 'sadistic but vulnerable' (2003: 24–25), and Gill Plain calls him 'predatory, menacing, emotionally detached, and yet also, paradoxically, [he] embodies an almost feminine beauty' (2006: 105). Adrian Garvey (2015, 2016) characterises him as a perverse patriarch defined more by attitude and voice than any visual sign, whilst for others his appeal lies in a resemblance to the Brontë's Heathcliff or Rochester.[1] Throughout, Mason's persona is that of a transgressive figure who mixes good and evil, romance and violence, rebelliousness and authority; handsomeness countered with a sneer, coupled with a voice part-velvet, part-strained and steely. Even in the thirty-plus years since his death, the image of the brooding, sinister, charming anti-hero prevails, and it is through this distinct persona that Mason's popular stardom has been most understood and examined.

This chapter will reflect on a series of different public identities and contexts around Mason and examine the relationship between the changing images and spaces of his star persona and his significance to scholarly studies of stardom. Ora Gelley (in relation to Ingrid Bergman) has highlighted how some critical analyses tend to take publicity discourse at face value, a strategy that then blocks critical readings of other elements (such as Bergman's films). She suggests that one impact of this is that critical readings too readily accept publicity material's assessment of a star's career (2008: 26). To some degree this is also true of Mason. But, as I will explore, much promotional material produced during Mason's long career constructed and circulated further public identities which critical analyses do not (or cannot) always acknowledge. In line with Gelley's critique, this analytical tactic tends to take the dominant Mason persona described above at face value, perhaps also limiting further critical readings. My aim here is to provide a space where these multiple identities can be examined along with the traditional conflicted 'Byronic' image, not just to show the complexity of his star persona but also how methodological frameworks influence our awareness of star personae. So this chapter is as much an exploration of critical contexts that investigate and reconstruct star meanings as it is of the features of Mason's persona through his own on- and off-screen identities.

The star they loved to hate

The idea of Mason as a complex star positioned between adoration and abhorrence is most identified with the release of the British Gainsborough Pictures melodrama *The Man in Grey* in 1943, and was consolidated by the roles that followed.[2] In the film, which is set in the Regency period, Mason plays the eponymous 'man in grey', Lord Rohan, a charismatic but cruel aristocratic, who – in need of an heir – marries the gentle Clarissa (Phyllis Calvert). Clarissa's callous best friend, Hester (Margaret Lockwood), uses this connection to her own advantage and begins an affair with Rohan. After Clarissa falls ill, Hester takes the opportunity to hasten the death of her friend so she may be free to marry Rohan. On discovering this, Rohan, incensed that she dared dishonour a member of the Rohan family, beats her to death.

The film was a major box-office success and propelled the main actors to stardom, with a particular focus on Mason as a brand-new home-grown star. Indicative of the scale of the star's popularity, Mark Glancy cites the 1944 results of the fan magazine *Picturegoer*'s annual readers' poll that awarded him and *The Man in Grey* the 'Gold Medal' in the category of actor and film, writing, 'Mason's starring role appeared to have overwhelmed the voters' (2011: 473). Mason made four more films for Gainsborough Pictures between 1943 and 1945, mainly in similarly sadistic roles, including *Fanny by Gaslight* (1944) as the villainous rake Lord Manderstoke, an abusive husband in *They Were Sisters* (1945) and highwayman Terry Jackson in *The Wicked Lady* (1945).[3] Mason loathed these films and his time at the studio, leaving in 1945 to work with producer Sydney Box on *The Seventh Veil*. Here, Mason played Nicholas, the bitter and crippled guardian

The Man in Grey (1943)

of Francesca (Ann Todd), a talented young pianist. The film is told mainly in flashback following a suicide attempt by Francesca as she recalls Nicholas' attempts to control every aspect of her life, loves and career. This culminates in an explosion of jealous rage during which he strikes her hands repeatedly and she flees from him. Undergoing psychotherapy with Dr Larsen (Herbert Lom), Francesca discovers that her true love is not one of her past suitors, but Nicholas, whose love for her is equally strong. Although this could be generically categorised as another psychological melodrama where he played another seemingly cruel and violent authoritarian, it was a film that Mason rated far higher than his Gainsborough pictures in terms of personal satisfaction and intelligent approach to its subject, especially in its theme of psychoanalysis. It was also an even greater financial triumph than his Gainsborough films in both the UK and the United States, and Nicholas' combination of sadistic violence and romantic appeal further cemented Mason's star status and image. As an international hit and critical success, the film ultimately paved the way for his work on a very different type of film, *Odd Man Out*, his emigration to Hollywood and his absence from British cinema for over a decade.

From Mason's breakthrough in *The Man in Grey* to the end of his Gainsborough contract, the Rank Organisation (who owned Gainsborough) deliberately restructured the studio's production plan, developing films to exploit his popularity in these types of roles (Spicer 2003: 25). Publicity material circulated in the UK and abroad heavily marketed the star as 'the man you love to hate' (Morley 1989: 57), and it is this identity that persists in public and scholarly discourse. Forty years on (and more), two British television retrospectives introduce Mason in virtually the same way, with a distinct emphasis on Rohan, Nicholas and similar characters. Granada's *James Mason: The Star They Loved to Hate*, produced in 1984 (the year of his death), explained Mason's popularity through his roles as 'a new kind of screen hero; mean, sadistic, but undeniably sexy', whilst BBC2's *Talking Pictures* series (2013) identified his appeal as a 'cool anti-hero that audiences loved to hate ... with looks that made him a natural leading man and a voice that made him the perfect movie scoundrel'.

Evidence that these qualities were intrinsic to the appeal of Mason for audiences in the 1940s can be found in the empirical responses of female audiences at the time, especially in reference to *The Man in Grey* and *The Seventh Veil*. They highlight that uneasy sense of attraction, with one fan stating, 'To this day, I can recall the sexual allure of James Mason who walked with a limp and looked out from the screen with a serious scowl, a troubled presence waiting to be saved. Its presence provoked my own sense of loneliness and desire to be loved' (qtd. in Erens 1994: 26); and others continue in a similar vein: 'When the war started I was eleven and my idol was Tyrone Power. Now my other favourite is James Mason who I think is very seductive. I love his voice and his looks and I think he is very handsome. I don't know why I love him, but I know no one can take his place except Van Johnson' (qtd. in Morin 1960: 78); 'At night I kept seeing James Mason's face as he beat Hester to death. I could not get it out of my dreams for some time' (qtd. in Spicer 2003: 25). In bemused response to this popular image, Mason authored a satirical article for *Lilliput* magazine called 'Yes, I Beat My Wife' (undated [but circa 1945–46]). The words returned to haunt him, though, as this phrase was reworked in discourse that followed, prompting a further explanation in a short authorised biography (by friend John Monaghan) serialised in the *Sunday Graphic*: 'Yes, I beat my wife – the joke thousands believed: James Mason's answer to his fans' (Monaghan 1947). Mason continued to refer to himself through this image in interviews and press releases during his career in the United States, saying, 'No one plans to be the man-you-love-to-hate' (undated).

The contentious image of Mason as a man 'hated as much as loved' was also played out in the British press and centred around his off-screen personality. He was painted as a difficult star who openly loathed British films and filmmakers, even punching the director of

The Wicked Lady, Leslie Arliss, during filming (Macnab 2003). During 1945–46, the star wrote a number of polemical articles about the British film industry, including 'I hate producers!' (*Lilliput* magazine) and 'Why I am going to America' (*Winter Pie*). The most controversial was an article for *Summer Pie* magazine called 'Glamour', in which Mason ruminated on how working in theatre and film had changed his perception of the magic he had experienced as a spectator, whereby 'familiarity caused glamour to evaporate' (1945: page unknown). But this article also contained a sharp criticism of the British film industry: 'I find precious little glamour in British pictures … [it] would be a glum outlook for me if there were not still a Hollywood. And I do love my Hollywood' (ibid.). The article was challenged by professional filmmaking bodies (including The Association of Ciné Technicians and The British Film Producers Association) and reported widely by the press as sparking an argument with his employer J. Arthur Rank, with the *Daily Express* quoting Mason as saying, 'Arthur Rank is the worst thing that has happened to the British picture industry' (Anon. 1946). That this rejection of British cinema coincided with Mason's emigration to Hollywood at the end of 1946 was certainly noted. The press intensely scrutinised his career in America and responded with glee when it seemed to fail with headlines like 'Swelled head of James Mason' (Shepherd 1946) and 'What's gone wrong with James Mason?' (Lester 1950) which suggested that 'Mason's progress is in inverse ratio to his publicity'. There was disdain when it was reported that he was thinking of taking American citizenship, with the 'Man O'The People' column stating, 'Really, Mr Mason, I couldn't care less!' and presenting him as abandoning and 'belittling the community of his birth' (undated). And in 1952, on hearing that Mason was making a film in Europe, there was the emphatic commentary by Leonard Mosely in the *Daily Express* that '[Mason] will not be coming home. He can no longer, in the British sense, be considered ours.'

Therefore, intrinsic to Mason's persona is a specific context of 'the national', and this typically informs subsequent analyses of his image. From the literary traditions of the Byronic hero, to his controversial yet popular place in the British film industry, and to the daytime programming of British television which remembered him, Mason's relation to British culture and nostalgic responses to that form a stable framework through which we view and interpret his stardom. An understanding of his stardom is primarily important in so far as it informs studies of British national identity; he takes on significant cultural, ideological and national significance. The nature of Mason's conflicted and rebellious star persona (especially its dangerous sexuality) opens up key questions about the history and reception of British cinema and the relationship of film to a broader sense of desire, identity politics and cultural taste. Within works that explore this, key areas of investigation emerge and converge: the repositioning of culturally 'low' British films and genres as a significant part of national film history, particularly through psychoanalytic approaches to cinema, spectatorship and gender.[4] These accounts of Mason build upon wider explorations of British cinema, especially the place and function of Gainsborough melodrama throughout the 1940s.[5]

It is Mason's Gainsborough screen roles that form the basis for these psychoanalytic discussions, and through this his persona takes on a symbolic function that feeds into and supports analyses of those films as culturally important historical fantasies that enabled an escapism from the realism of war, home-front dramas, and their ideological function beyond this. As Marcia Landy writes, 'these films opened up vistas in relation to gender and sexuality that can hardly be dismissed as mere escapism' (2000: 65). In seeking to challenge their status as critically dismissed films, scholars explored how the Gainsborough melodramas were instrumental in providing discursive spaces for the representation of independent heroines who defied traditional patriarchal power, the breaking down of class barriers and the validation of hitherto unspoken erotic desires.[6] They configured these texts as conflicted spaces that enabled and often punished such transgression, displacing and disguising dialogues to both challenge class and gender roles *and* reaffirm patriarchal authority. In doing so they critically repositioned the films as raising significant questions about spectatorship and female audiences, whereby the pleasures of viewing are contained both in engaging with the image of aspirational emancipation and also a masochistic delight in the brutality of the vicious suppression meted out to resilient women by Mason's characters. Placed in such a filmic and critical context, Mason's persona becomes an embodiment of social concerns that are bound up in his transgressive, violent, sexy anti-heroes. He is a semiotic conduit for the anxiety of a nation, as Peter William Evans describes him, an exemplar of 'the return of the repressed of a nation', his persona embodying an id-driven release of libido, never innocent of ideology (2001: 116).

This leads to explorations of Mason's persona as an emblem of certain ideals and images of masculine identity that have been constructed through popular cinema. Through psychoanalytic and economic examinations of different male stars and their popular images, comparative analyses chart the range of different types of masculinity in British cinema of the 1940s and 1950s. Partly as a means of exploring more under-researched male stars, the established perceptions of the Gainsborough films and – subsequently – the development of Mason's persona mean that the star is used as a benchmark in these comparisons, helping to orientate other images of masculinity. He is often coupled with fellow 'sexual transgressor' Dirk Bogarde against the 'gentle dependables' Leslie Howard, Robert Donat and John Mills. Andy Medhurst aligns Bogarde and Mason through their shared 'erotic cruelty' but separates them on the grounds of class, citing how Mason's success in historical or aristocratic roles works in opposition to 'Bogarde's appropriation of the thrilling sadistic persona [as] urban, contemporary and working-class' (1986: 348). He is compared to John Mills by Geoffrey Macnab and Gill Plain in their explorations of Mills' 'everyman' image, where his ordinariness is constructed in contrast to Mason's exoticism, each author commenting on how Mills' popularity in Britain rose as Mason's fell.[7] Able to play across class barriers, Mills 'embodied decency and quiet heroism ... and toppled aristocratic cad and rotter, James Mason, from his perch at the top of the popularity polls in the mid-1940s' (Macnab 2000: 102), taking on 'the burden of national representation' (Plain 2006: 13) from the late 1940s. Both implicitly repeat public opinion of Mason as 'unpatriotic' in their observation that, when given the chance to move to Hollywood – unlike Mason – Mills remained in Britain, continuing to 'speak to and for the nation' (Plain 2006: 104). The ways in which national identity can be explored and measured through popular stardom, be it through gender, fiscal success or class ideals, lie at the heart of these discussions. Mason's star persona falls at the extreme: his British stardom is characterised by immense commercial success, aggressive and transgressive masculinity, a privileged class and his rejection of nation.[8] But, as I will explore in the following sections, even though these elements continue to inform dominant critical perceptions of Mason, to a large degree they all dissipate from other public constructions of him on and off screen as his career, private life and star image continue to unfold.

It should be noted though that certain elements were already 'absent' from public constructions of Mason's persona in the late 1930s and early 1940s. Mason's own autobiography, written in 1981, and Sheridan Morley's biography from 1989 chart two potentially scandalous elements from his pre-stardom life that remain absent from official circulation once his star rose. The first was his decision to register as a conscientious objector during World War II (his application was rejected and he was placed into non-combatant service). Continuous acting work allowed him to apply for deferment of call-up throughout the early 1940s, and Morley notes that whilst openly discussed within the profession, 'James did not at this point have a wide public following and his decision not to fight did not attract headlines' (1989: 50). The second was another open secret within the industry: that before Mason married his first wife, Pamela Kellino, in

1941, he moved in with her and her then husband Roy Kellino (circa 1937). This was no mere lodging arrangement, but an odd love triangle that both Mason and Morley find hard to describe. Mason admits that 'technically I was a bachelor, but morally – if that is the right word – I was married to Pamela Kellino' (1981: 154), whilst Morley writes that 'James, in his characteristically clenched and embarrassed way ... wrote only that "I was very attracted to Pamela, and went to live with her husband for several years before we were married"' (1989: 35).

These early years, where Mason's private world contained such transgressive elements as a love life that openly rejected conventional morality and an unpatriotic act of non-combat status, could have easily further informed a persona reliant on conflict, non-conformist sexuality and an uneasy relationship with the national. But they can also be seen to *destabilise* that persona, reconstructing Mason in more passive terms than existing discourse otherwise suggests. The considered pacifism complicates the identity of the impulsive, brutal sadist; the unfussy co-habiting (and the unsophisticated way this is remembered) renders Mason as a naive man anxious to avoid conflict and uncomfortable discussing sexuality. Peter William Evans briefly touches on the conscientious objection in the introduction to his chapter on Mason, explaining it as indicative of the actor's wider personal anxieties before moving on to concentrate on his sadistic appeal. Mason himself is quite evasive on both counts, obscuring true reflection within rather opaque prose, so it is difficult to approach the subjects in a wholly archival sense. Additionally, I am sure the Rank Organisation did much to ensure that neither history was revisited as public scandal as Mason's stardom grew; the need to *love* Mason was at least as important as the need to *hate* him. However, these private circumstances remain interesting addendums to that persona in the way they support *and* subvert it, yet remain relatively absent in comparison to other textual, biographical and analytical detail. As one obituary puts it, Mason remained 'a star of magnetism and menace' and it is 'the clutch of black and white British melodramas on which his claim to be remembered will rest' (Russell 1984).

The odd man out

Beyond British mainstream cinema of the mid-1940s, the cultural, filmic, national and historical contexts that surrounded the star all changed significantly. This led to the development of Mason's persona where the paradoxes and conflicts contained within it extend beyond the 'charismatically dangerous' to one that placed him as a figure out-of-place and out-of-time. Articles, retrospectives and critical analyses reconfigure 'The Man You Love to Hate' as the 'Odd Man Out'. The magnetism and menace of his earlier films remain central to discourse around Mason's persona, but whilst initially his public image drew heavily on his on-screen professional life, with some focus on his insolent attitude off screen, as time progressed, his off-screen life began to play a greater part in supporting (and then challenging) the wider meanings of his star persona. This is partly because after 1945 – although still publicly associated with certain characters – Mason's actual screen work employed him in many different types of roles throughout the late 1940s and 1950s. Retrospectively, the difficulties in casting he seemed to face in Hollywood suggest a more complex engagement with employment, role and performance, but from a more conventional perspective, this signalled wasted opportunities and a career in freefall. Here, the traditional narrative constructs him as a star who turned his back on Britain to seek further fortune in glamorous Hollywood, and whose apparent failure to capitalise on his position as Britain's most popular male star left him without star identity and without nation, his persona positioned within contexts of emigration and existentialist angst.

In terms of both Mason's career and critical analyses of the actor, the turning point is Carol Reed's 1947 film *Odd Man Out*, which depicts the last hours of Johnny McQueen (Mason), an IRA leader wounded and on the run in Belfast.[9] Shot and slowly dying after a disastrous robbery, Johnny weakly negotiates the city and its characterful inhabitants as police and friends frantically search for him. The journey is framed with themes of religion, morality and duty, exploring these from a metaphysical and philosophical (rather than political) viewpoint. Finally reaching his beloved Kathleen (Kathleen Ryan), he is unable to make the boat passage to freedom, and they are both gunned down by the police. As with *The Seventh Veil*, *Odd Man Out* was commercially successful and critically acclaimed on both sides of the Atlantic – further showing the potential of Mason as an international star.

Critical examinations of the film emphasise its relations to thematic concerns found throughout Reed's career, emphasising how it traces the psychology of its subject through Johnny's existential crisis in the face of death and punishment. Roger Manvell noted that 'the gravity of the film's theme ... is the revelation of human qualities against the final measure of good and evil' (qtd. in Morley 1989: 72), and Mason's casting worked in service of these themes, with *The New York Times* observing that 'Mason gives a terrifying picture of a wounded man' (Hirschhorn 1977: 83). His handsomeness emphasises the romantic fragility of a tragic hero deserving of pathos; his transgressive masculinity adds a further underlying darkness to the film. The sense of identity created around Johnny as the film's thematic focus also signals shifts in considerations of Mason's stardom: the exciting aggression of his earlier image is transfigured into the 'doomed masculinity' that Peter William Evans and others – such as Amy Lawrence (2010) – read the rest of his career through (2001: 115). It is Evans who most thoroughly articulates the film as a psychological and philosophical text in both his chapter on the star (2001) and the extended analysis in his book devoted to Carol Reed (2005). In his earlier chapter, the Gainsborough-created 'monstrous sadist' dominates his argument, but within this Evans identifies a self-destructive element to Mason's persona. He is seen to occupy an outsider status, a site through which existential angst can be identified and meditated on. In examining his Hollywood films of the 1950s, Evans suggests that 'the Mason character's violence against self and others seems informed in a popularised way by contemporary

Odd Man Out (1947)

existential angst mixed … with Sade' (2001: 116). Evans' 2005 analysis of Reed's film mirrors this closely, albeit through an auteurist lens that focuses on Johnny's character rather than Mason's persona. Evans discusses how the decay of Johnny's body and mind expresses wider analyses of the unconscious mind, the impossibility of the present and the fragmentation of identity (2005: 67). By the end, he offers a brief analysis of Mason's persona through Johnny, arguing that in making its protagonist a dying passive spectator, *Odd Man Out* self-reflexively subverts Mason's image, rescuing it from its former sexual obsession and pre-empting Hitchcock's employment of it in *North by Northwest*. In the earlier chapter, the idea of subversion is downplayed in favour of presenting a more coherent account of a singular persona: existential violence against 'self *and* others'. However, what is suggested here, through the psychological reading of film and director, is a distinct shift in the construction and use of Mason's persona on screen.

In his deconstruction of Mason's persona, Evans comments on the apparent link between private self and public image in how he approached his characters from *Odd Man Out* onwards, suggesting that they are similarly imbued with the actor's own passivity, angst and sense of shortcomings, particularly in terms of how his career in Hollywood developed (2001: 115). And it is *Odd Man Out*'s status as Mason's 'last British film as major British star' that takes on significance within this.[10] It is a literal and symbolic departure from Mason's British life. Its mournful tone, expressionistic style and tragic theme mark it apart from the historical melodramas he despised so much, and on its completion Mason and family made the long sea crossing to New York. Expatriated from the UK, the actor followed a long line of British and European emigrants to Hollywood during the 1940s. As mentioned earlier, the British press reported this relocation in negative terms – firstly as a rejection of country and then as a failed career. Mason records that he never felt completely at home in Hollywood, and after the end of the 1950s he worked in a variety of European cinemas and locales, later settling in Switzerland. It is this narrative that informs elements of Mason's public identity: that of a man who does not (and cannot) ever 'belong', metaphorically banished to the most neutral of spaces. Whilst his emigration was presented at the time in aggressively negative terms, in retrospectives written with hindsight this story is used to elegiacally reconstruct Mason as a tragic figure who was doomed to roam the wilderness, denied access to nation through his rejection of Britain in 1947, and access to stardom through his failed Hollywood career and movement into character roles.

That this narrative can be signified so fittingly by the title of and themes present in *Odd Man Out* is never missed, and the meaning of 'James Mason' seems inextricably bound up in that film and its contexts. Five years after the actor's death, Sheridan Morley assuredly used the film as the title of his 1989 biography, Paul Ward's (2013) recent analysis draws on the phrase, as does

Christopher Sandford's 2009 profile. More obliquely, Peter William Evans' chapter refers to the *other* film Mason made with Reed, *The Man Between* (1953), but equally a film of lost spaces and identities, it hints at the earlier film. The precedent of such an explicit connection between the personal and professional originated from British journalist Olga Franklin in the mid-1950s in her article for the *Daily Sketch* entitled 'James Mason: odd man out' (1953) and was continued in the headlines of Mason's obituaries from 1984: 'The odd man out who became a legend' (Hellicar 1984); 'Odd man out – the one role James Mason never quite lost' (Jones 1984). Later feature articles publicising re-releases of Mason's films maintained the trend: 'James Mason: superstar who was an odd man out' (Richards 1990); 'Odd man out … the contradictions of James Mason' (Macnab 2003). These articles and obituaries revisit and re-evaluate Mason's career and performances. They recount his belligerent attitude to British filmmaking, reflect on the singular quality of *Odd Man Out*, chart a troubled time in Hollywood with moments of brilliance (although here they differ in opinion – depending on which author, either *Lolita* or *A Star Is Born* [1954] or *Julius Caesar* [1953]), and the somewhat disappointing final act of his life as a supporting actor. In all, his star status is bound to nation, split between the career before *Odd Man Out* and the career after, where he was forever chasing the popularity of the sadistic yet magnetic persona of his Gainsborough anti-heroes.

Through the constant reworking of Mason as an 'odd man out', his public image remains tied to one in constant conflict with himself and others: the personification of the 'outsider' as professional failure, existentialist hero and as a subject lacking in the security of nation. Such definitions suggest continuities with wider scholarly discourse around European émigrés in Hollywood cinema, where, as I have explored elsewhere, the tragic narrative is one often invoked to describe the transatlantic journey of stars, filmmakers and other artists (Thomas 2012). The historical and cultural analysis of exiles and émigrés is a popular approach to studies of national and transnational cinemas, and as James Morrison's comments in his seminal work on the subject, 'Europe' and 'America' have been conceptualised as symbolic cultural and oppositional spaces of European art, elitism, tradition verses American commerce, democracy, mass culture (1998: 2). The field also tends to foreground politically motivated emigration (around World War II), the stylistic and thematic influence of European filmmakers in Hollywood (especially on film noir and other existentialist cinemas), and economic relationships between institutionalised national cinemas (through production facilities and distribution networks).[11] Some elements of Mason's stardom fit neatly into the concept of cultural opposition, particularly in terms of perceptions of success, his upper-class standing, his conflicted persona and – through *Odd Man Out* – expressionist artful cinema. But other aspects of his life make the star much harder to categorise within the above topics – such as a stardom formed through commercial films, his relocation only after the war, or Hollywood casting that made little of him as an emblematic representation of Britain (unlike David Niven or Ronald Colman) – rendering it more difficult to place Mason in critical histories of stars' roles in political, cultural and economic exchange.

Where he can be found in works on the interconnectedness between Hollywood and Europe is in Robert Murphy's chapter on British film noir in *European Film Noir* (2007), a volume designed to challenge noir as a European-influenced, but decidedly American cinema. Murphy uses Mason in a similar way to the genre studies of Gainsborough melodrama: his roles are briefly positioned as typical of the genre in their sadism and doomed masculinity. In doing so, Murphy implicitly continues to reinforce this as the main way of understanding Mason's stardom, although the films prioritised – *The Night Has Eyes* (1942) and *The Upturned Glass* (1947) – are less well known than the noirish *Odd Man Out* but still in line with the overall emphasis of uncovering an untold history of European cinema.

Thus, Murphy raises questions about how readings of Mason's stardom have concentrated on his most widely circulated films: those that fit most with the dominant persona. But even in the period and industry he is most associated with, Mason made other British films (before and after becoming a star) with many production companies, including (as well as those cited by Murphy) *Late Extra* (1935 Fox), *The Mill on the Floss* (1936 G. B. Morgan), his own independent production *I Met a Murderer* (1939), *This Man is Dangerous* (1941 Rialto/Pathé), *Hatter's Castle* (1941 Paramount British), *Alibi* (1942 British Lion), *Secret Mission* (1942 Excelsior), *Thunder Rock* (1942 MGM), *The Bells Go Down* (1943 Ealing), *They Met in the Dark* (1943 Excelsior), *Candlelight in Algeria* (1943 British Lion), *Hotel Reserve* (1944 RKO) and *A Place of One's Own* (1945 Gainsborough). In these films, he played both leading and peripheral roles, and a variety of characters, some still sadistic, but others who are more conventional romantic heroes or supporting types. Many of these films are not readily available. In 2010, *This Man is Dangerous* was included on the BFI's Most Wanted list of lost British films; *Candlelight in Algeria* was released on DVD in 2007 by the online distribution company Odeon Entertainment, who specialise in forgotten classics of British cinema; and *The Mill on the Floss* was released on DVD only in 2014. *Hatter's Castle*, *The Bells Go Down* and *Thunder Rock* are available, but Mason only has minor roles and little screen time. Within analyses of stardom, further consideration of the accessibility of film texts and the value of supporting roles need to be more fully taken into account, especially, as it is often argued, the significance of Mason's 'nationally symbolic' star persona is simply the result of restricted casting in one type of film, which frustrated him so much he rebelled against a whole industry and nation. It also negates the cross-national work he continued to do after 1947 – from writing articles for the British press from Hollywood to the transatlantic journeys he made to film *Pandora and the Flying Dutchman* (1951) at Shepperton Studios, London, and to Berlin for *The Man Between*.

The celebritisation of the Masons

With a persona forged through his British career of the 1940s, there is a tendency to read Mason's post-1950 roles through that image. However, here I want to focus on an alternative image that existed in public discourse throughout the decade following his arrival in America: an image (and narrative) of excess born from the intense 'celebritisation' of Mason and his family. I use that term to show how Mason's identity in the United States relied far more on the private/public sphere – his off-screen antics as reported in the press through publicity and gossip – rather than through his professional screen roles. Therefore, here, I reposition readings of his star persona away from the traditional examinations of his stardom where the central question extends from the star's semiotic significance to the film text and wider cultural identity. Mason's screen characters appear to be less significant here (partly because they did not repeat the same apparent typecasting), and throughout his Hollywood career his screen function was varied (from lead to support, hero to antagonist, narrator to ensemble player), as were his roles. These included the sharp but kind romantic hero in *Caught* (1949), sympathetic hood in *The Reckless Moment* (1949), playboy murder suspect in *East Side, West Side* (1949), ghostly lover in *Pandora and the Flying Dutchman*, Nazi officer in *The Desert Fox* (1951), ageing troubled star in *A Star Is Born*, guardian angel in *Forever Darling* (1956), teacher-turned-addict in *Bigger Than Life* (1956), ordinary family man in *Cry Terror!* (1958), eccentric adventurer in *Journey to the Centre of the Earth* (1959), sexually tempted professor in *The Marriage-Go-Round* (1961), and many more. Instead, it is Mason and his unconventional family that garners extensive headlines.

Ironically, the first headlines came from Mason's apparent reluctance to engage with the Hollywood publicity machine. The imminent arrival of the major British star meant that stories circulated in the gossip columns even before he set foot onshore, and the first wave perpetuated the negative views of the British press. As Mason records, due to the immense interest in his move to Hollywood, the infamous gossip columnist Louella Parsons repeatedly tried to arrange an exclusive interview with the star, but John Monaghan (friend, biographer and at this time acting as press agent) mistakenly refused to grant her an interview (1981: 234). Deeply affronted, Parsons denounced the 'uncooperative' Mason on her nationally broadcast radio show. In an attempt to rectify the damage, Mason and his wife Pamela formed a close alliance with Parsons' rival Hedda Hopper, who by the mid-1950s had a syndicated newspaper column with an estimated daily readership of 32 million. It was swiftly agreed that if the Masons had 'any titbits of personal news to dispose of, the obvious thing would be to toss them to Hopper' (ibid.: 236). Jennifer Frost notes Hopper's power and success in mounting public campaigns for and against certain stars (2011: 2), and finding himself stuck between the bitter gossip rivals and in constant circulation, the star became – at least according to him – a reluctant celebrity. His wife, however, took on the role with far more gusto and reportedly became the main driving force behind their many public appearances. On arrival in the United States, Mason and Pamela became a double act of sorts, with public appearances across media sites, gossip columns and even on screen, and, as the 1950s progressed, to a large degree in the eyes of the American public, a singular identity of 'James Mason' did not exist. If he was present, so was his whole family: wife, children and cats.

The children came later, but the cats are initially *very* important. By the time he left Britain, Mason had accrued many pets – most of them cats – and they all made the Atlantic crossing together. The American press became fascinated with the image of a Noah-like Mason leading a menagerie across the sea and country (unable to take them by train, they drove to Los Angeles by ambulance). The *Life* magazine feature announcing his arrival peppered the article with images of the cats – in travel cases at the docks and, later, settled into the Masons' study. In a letter to Hopper, Pamela relayed the 'titbit' tale of one cat's sickness (1946), and features by the journalists Gladys Hall (undated) and Jack Hirshberg (1948, 1949) all mention them, as does a Twentieth Century-Fox 1947 biography (Anon.). The cats can be seen as a means of sidestepping the star's brutal image for a more positive, relatable one, as illustrated by Mason's radio appearance on *The Burns & Allen Show* (1949), where conversation is swiftly shifted from beatings to felines, with George Burns reprimanding Gracie Allen's description of Mason as a 'magnificent monster', arguing 'Mason is not that type of man. As a matter of fact, his hobby is raising cats.' It was an image partly cultivated by the Masons themselves – most notably in 1949 when he and Pamela authored a book reflecting on their pets called *The Cats in Our Lives*.

Whilst on the one hand this public image was domestic and accessible, it also conveyed aspects that countered this. The initial press fascination obviously identified something odd and exotic in the star's menagerie (Mason: 'So we liked cats. What was so strange … about that?' [1981: 266]). Mason tired quickly of being presented as a cat-obsessive, writing a few years later, 'the reading public may now relax … without fear of encountering some idiot reference to the Mason cats [in the press]' (1950) and revealing that *The Cats in Our Lives* came from financial necessity, being a venture that would have high and swift returns at a time when their assets were stretched (1981: 266). What is most evident through the range of archival material is the diverse personas with which Mason was becoming associated. It had continuities with the British persona with regard to his rudeness and the strangeness of his appeal, but the exoticness was very different. Rather than continuing as a complex desiring of erotically brutal masculinity or an underlying femininity figured through tragic beauty, the exoticness was conveyed in a more objective way, where a fascinated public wryly viewed an odd domestic bliss. And it did persist, even in the UK; years later, the *Sunday Express* reported the Masons' divorce in 1964 with the headline 'At 55, Mr Mason faces up to life without Pam and the cats' (Anon. 1964).

Pamela was certainly an intrinsic part of Mason's Hollywood identity, and whilst the presence of a wife helped domesticate his image, her perpetual company proved to be a contentious one. From the start, publicity material presented them as a package; their press representative Constance Sykes delivered 'a hand-out on the MASONS' to Hopper in 1946, and articles in the US and UK press almost always mentioned both of them. But Pamela was often presented as a corrosive influence on Mason's reputation, particularly through her unsuccessful attempts to maintain a career on the back of his (including their appearance together in the portmanteau film *Charade* [1953]). Interviews also tended to mock her, with Jack Hirshberg's article describing 'the incessant babble of [Mason's] actress-author-publicist-wife ... who talks too much and says too little' (1948), and an *Evening Standard* piece that presented Mason as a hen-pecked husband, noting that the star 'took a gulp of tea [and] looked at his wife for agreement' when asked if he felt successful in Hollywood (Conway 1950). In a later interview, Pamela offended the Hollywood elite with her sketch of its different cliques: 'I guess we're not chi-chi enough to make that smart, ultra-British set ... Then there are the breeders ... the executive-and-money set ... the bachelorette set ... culture vultures ... and the Bohemians' (Morley 1989: 99). Forced to issue a public apology, the Masons' reputation as a celebrity couple whose main source of fame seemed to come only from bad publicity grew. Despite Mason's self-professed image of the reluctant celebrity, Hirshberg wrote that 'he loves to stir up comment ... basically Mason is a man who likes headlines and is sufficiently canny to know what editors will print' (1949).

This celebrity status continued with a growing interest in Mason's children – daughter Portland (b. 1948) and son Morgan (b. 1955) – especially Portland, who became known as 'the world's most precocious child' and after whom Mason named his production company, Portland Pictures (Anon. 2004a).[12] Portland soon overtook the cats as the star's preferred topic for interviewers: 'there are nine cats now, but Portland is her father's favourite ...' (Franklin: undated). Portland also became a contentious figure: she pursued an acting career partly through Mason's contacts and financing, appearing briefly in *Bigger Than Life*, *The Man in the Gray Flannel Suit* (1956) and *The Great St. Trinian's Train Robbery* (1966), but this was overshadowed by controversial tales of her upbringing and questions about the Masons' parenting skills. Reportedly, by the age of three, Portland had already tried smoking and kept unsociable hours, staying up until midnight and sleeping all morning (ibid.), and a year later had her own mink fur coat (Hirschhorn 1969).[13] Aged seven, she was a constant presence at cocktail parties, including one where she 'spontaneously jumped on stage and did a burlesque dance routine, complete with grinds, that left Dean Martin speechless' (Irvin 2010: 220). In 1954, she made *The Child* (1954), a short film directed by Mason and written by Pamela, prompting *The Hollywood Reporter* to comment, 'Portland Mason as a child? Talk about miscasting!' (Anon. 2004b). Reports of a decadent and spoiled childhood were greeted with glee in the American newspapers and grimly in the British press as further evidence of how far Mason had fallen from grace. In the mid-1950s, Olga Franklin interviewed shoppers from Mason's home town of Huddersfield who knew more about Portland and her behaviour than they did about Mason himself, with one local quoted as being 'shocked' at how she was being raised with 'late dinners and high talk instead of her bottom being smacked and [sent] off to bed' (undated).

Reviewing this material, there is a contemporaneous feel to the narrative of the Masons' celebrity status and association with excess. Elements of it seem like an early attempt at the pursuit, promotion and branding of a 'star family' more closely linked with contemporary celebrity value. The intense press interest in Mason's daughter is a precursor to the huge financial value attributed to images and gossip of celebrity families such as the Jolie-Pitts by the modern tabloid press. The financial strategy of rebranding individual stars into a coherent and profitable 'family identity', where one or two major stars position their children and/or spouse as central parts of their public image, is also discussed as a key feature of contemporary global stardom. Paul McDonald cites the example of how the already multimedia/cross synergy image of Will Smith has been transferred across to his wife and children (Jada Pinkett Smith, Jaden and Willow Smith) (2013: 176), whilst Marie-Agnes Parmentier's examination of the importance of the branding of David and Victoria Beckham and their children to stakeholders (2011), not to mention the significant rise of the Kardashian family as a hugely profitable exercise in branding and circulation through images of excess – and it is useful to consider Mason's star persona in light of this.

It is also indicative of new critical approaches to celebrity and consumer culture which explore different types of stars as sites of unwanted excess and promotion to enable a wider analysis of public consumption and the self (Marshall 2010: 35). In 2000, Christine Geraghty argued for a re-evaluation of the way film stars may be positioned within critical landscapes, where 'the term celebrity indicates someone whose fame rests overwhelmingly on what happens outside their sphere of work and who is famous for having a lifestyle' (99). Given the importance of Mason's film roles to the establishment of his persona, and the later acclaimed reputation as an actor/star through his 1950s Hollywood films, it is notable how absent his film work becomes in discourses of fame during this period. Both Marshall and Geraghty explore celebrity culture as a recent modification in contemporary stardom and the development of celebrity studies as the necessary critical reflection of this. However, acknowledging the excessive celebritisation of the Masons as a family brand, and an analysis of the repositioning of Mason's persona during the 1950s as one overly reliant on his private family life, does complicate the implied location of 'celebrity' as a primarily modern phenomenon, arising from changing dynamics within contemporary stardom.

As such, the significance of deconstructing Mason's persona can be extended beyond the singular cultural image created by his

British screen roles of the 1940s. It becomes more pertinent to include the image of the oddball, cat-obsessed, bohemian family unit in our understanding of his stardom, even though it relates little to the earlier image in its reliance on the brand identity of The Masons. Elements of transgression and conflict still figure, but are of a very different nature. Here, his celebrity status is much less coherent than the Byronic image of the previous decade but was just as much part of Mason's public persona for audiences in the 1950s and in the USA and UK. Although well known at the time, the star's public image during his Hollywood career is a difficult identity to situate easily and, as a result, it has been underplayed when examining the nature of his stardom and persona. However, in addition to further revealing the complexity of his star status, taking the celebritisation of James Mason seriously contributes to a wider discussion around the necessary historicisation of the 'celebrity' (especially the male celebrity) within film and entertainment industries in general.

Youth reborn, or the prodigal Yorkshireman

In my last analysis of the multiple identities that informed Mason's star persona, I continue to follow Mason's classification of his career through a 'three-act structure', citing *Lolita* (1962) as the turning point that introduced the final act (Stott 1969). For Mason, Kubrick's film was significant, as it marked a repatriation to the UK and the start of a new and settled life. His 1981 autobiography ends soon after this moment, though, giving the impression that he has little else to say about those years. Elsewhere, elegiac retrospectives use the period briefly to reconstruct Mason as the prodigal son; the contrite star reconciling with his homeland after the reckless and wasteful extravagances of Hollywood, and maturing into a distinguished but low-key status as 'one of cinema's finest character actors, so consistently good … that you tended to forget sometimes how good he was' (Richards 1990). The theme of the forgotten and the invisible permeates this late discourse: one year before his death, he is referred to as 'The nearly man' (Lewin 1983: 69), someone who 'never quite achieved the peaks he had sought' (Anon. 1984), and 'a star of the sidelines' (Gilbey 2003). All this add credence to analyses that articulate Mason's star persona through a publicly played out tragic narrative communicated through themes of anger, doom and loss. But here I emphasise those 'forgotten' years, also acknowledging how methodological approaches have developed ways of engaging with stars through studies of regional identity and television, audiences and oral history, and ageing.

His divorce from Pamela in 1964, and marriage to Clarissa in 1971, contributed to Mason's belief that he had entered a new phase of his life, and that despite growing into a mature age, he felt he retained a 'juvenile optimism' (Lewin 1983: 69). Away from the pressures of celebrity and attempting to manage a traditional star status in leading roles, the conflict, excess and transgression that had previously characterised the Mason persona seemed to dissipate. As with his career in the 1950s, the types of characters he was cast as varied immensely during these years (see Chapter 3). A laissez-faire attitude to his work could also be observed, where judgments on quality were less important than location and schedule, as indicated in his rejection letter to director Daniel Mann on being offered *Lost in the Stars* (1974): 'I ask myself what's in it for me and the computer answers "a free trip to Israel, what more do you want?" The trouble is, I've never been that keen to go to Israel' (1973). Interviews chart an astonishment that the arrogant and 'once so-ferocious' Mason had become 'a very mellow fellow', no longer irritated by Rank, Hollywood, Pamela, the cats, or indeed journalists (Mann 1967). Now in his sixties, 'his nature has become as mellow as his voice, his eyebrows beetle into a smile instead of a ferocious scowl' (Anon. 1975). His countenance is now 'positively avuncular ... secure in the knowledge that his professional standing has never been higher' (Mann 1983). Rather than presenting himself as ageing and slowing down, these are the years of the actor's 're-birth' (Stott 1969) and 'rejuvenation' (Anon. 1968).

This representation places Mason somewhat at odds with conventional conceptions of ageing and stardom, an area of investigation that Chris Holmlund argues forms 'one of the key tasks confronting celebrity studies today' (2010: 96). Much of the early appeal of Mason was attributed to his sexual appeal and attractiveness. His co-star Geraldine Fitzgerald remembered him as 'incredibly good-looking, in a dark sort of way' (qtd. in Morley 1989: 37), Gill Plain describes his 'feminine beauty' and Richard Corliss gives an account of his 'sepulchral beauty' (qtd. in Lawrence 2010: 88). The much-admired beauty of his younger years should place Mason alongside similarly *beautifully male* stars such as Cary Grant, Montgomery Clift, Marlon Brando, Alain Delon and James Dean. Each of these stars communicates a particular circumstance of ageing which then informs perceptions and analyses of their star personas: Dean's early death meant he didn't age, Brando's weight gain obscured his beauty and Grant retreated from public view. Clift's facial disfigurement meant his stardom became emblematic of the decay of youth (McNally 2012), and Delon's obvious ageing is typical of the poignancy with which beautiful stars carry memories of their younger selves (Vincendeau 2000: 181).[14]

As he grew older, Mason stood apart from modes of ageing constructed through trauma and decay. Through his career, there was no ontological shock of death, ruin or the reveal of sudden change that affected his public image. Mason aged steadily and in continuous view, prompting one interviewer to note that 'He has aged as he has lived, gracefully and discreetly' (Lowry 1981). The roundness of his face maintained a healthy appearance and his voice remained as recognisable as it ever was, silky and sharp. 'Mason is now a beautiful old man … his face glows with a yearning and bemused innocence …' (Kroll qtd. in Morley 1989: 167). It is also this beauty that separates Mason from non-destructive images of other modes of male ageing,

North by Northwest (1959)

where the discursive circulation of (mostly white) older male stars signifies their ageing as an exhibition of a positive, powerful middle age (Holmlund 2010: 98). Through their shared appearance in *North by Northwest*, Adrian Garvey (2016) contrasts Mason with the (on-screen) powerful ideal of ageing symbolised by Grant and notes that whilst Grant's 'ideal' could last only a few years more, Mason's career seemed to rejuvenate as he aged.

Mason's attitude to and embodiment of an image of 'non-ageing' also connects to the idea that the public performance of ageing marks the potential for individual transformation, that a refusal to 'act one's age' forms a space where 'individuals have the chance to rebecome what they once were … or wish to have become' (Swinnen 2012: 10). The absence from Mason's public ageing of the traditional stereotypes of decline or power, as well as his own self-professed identity of rejuvenation – where the prospect of his career was exciting and 'more fun [now] than in the early years' (Anon. 1967a) – suggests a refusal to succumb to conventional old age. This is present in some of his on-screen roles, especially in the energetic performances and/ or rebellious characters in the comedies of the late 1950s and early 1960s, and again in *Age of Consent*, *Cold Sweat* (1970), *Kill!* (1971) and *The Last of Sheila* (1973). Behind-the-scenes stories reveal more, with journalist Ian Black recalling the filming of *The Yin and Yang of Mr Go* (1970) where Mason, 'the apparently very buttoned-up English gentleman [sat] in a hotel room, smoking a joint and reading from James Joyce' (Morley 1989: 154). Bernard Gordon, producer of *Bad Man's River* (1971), remembers picking up the actor at the airport prior to filming:

He was not the clean shaven, bowler-hatted gentleman in impeccable Bond Street attire I had expected. He had long unkempt hair, wore a casual shirt and trousers that looked like they had been slept in for a month … I had to assume he was in his hippie mode. It was 1971 after all. (1999: 255)

Both stories mention Clarissa; clearly – in distinct contrast to Pamela – a mellowing influence on her husband. At least in part, the older Mason presented himself through youthful discourse and, in doing so, disrupted social type and expectation; and whilst not conveyed through his literal physical ageing, this was nonetheless a transformative moment in his already transgressive public persona.

The film roles of this later period reflect the notion that as he aged, Mason was ready to experiment with new experiences. This began even before *Lolita* in British, American and European films from the late 1950s onwards, although it comes into sharper focus after Kubrick's film. Pre-empting the blackly comic elements of *Lolita* in 1962, Mason had already explored more broadly comic leading roles in *A Touch of Larceny* (1959) and *The Marriage-Go-Round*, and this would continue with *Age of Consent*. These and other roles played upon – and with – subjects of sexuality, extending beyond the erotic brutality/doomed romanticism of the younger image of Mason. He became the dashing military rogue in *Larceny* and *Tiara Tahiti* (1962), a married intellectual unsure how to deal with the advances of a young bombshell in *Marriage*, and the uninterested object of female attention in *Age of Consent*. In all of these, there is an inherent ridiculousness to the attractions as well as an understanding of them. The use of Mason to explore a variety of contemporary sexual mores continued in a more dramatic vein when the star was cast in lead and supporting roles as an exemplar of awkward yearning attempting to escape from traditions of socially permissible behaviour and the emotional pain or grotesque bitterness of powerless cuckolded husbands in comedy drama *Georgy Girl* (1966), spy thriller *The Deadly Affair* and realist drama *The Pumpkin Eater* (1964). The style and subject of these films signals that Mason was in the process of aligning himself towards a more contemporary film landscape, particularly associated with British cinema of the 1960s. The subsequent sexualised image of him in these films develops the complexity of Mason as a differently desired and desiring figure, in turn challenging an audience's expectation of the star and adding to the uneasy tone of each film.

The new British cinema of the 1960s has long been associated with opening up boundaries of realist aesthetics, subject matter, class and geography. Crucial to this was an initial construction of representations of 'The North' and the working class, often utilising unknown Northern actors from the stage to help achieve this sense of realism and challenge existent trends of older British cinema. Although *Georgy Girl* is set in London, Mason used a Yorkshire accent in his portrayal of the wealthy industrialist James Leamington, and beyond this, the mid-1960s marked a significant reconnection with the North by Mason, both on screen and off, especially with his home town of Huddersfield. Regional identity became one of the dominant images of Mason during his later years, where he continually presented himself – and was presented by others – as a proud Yorkshireman, anxious to communicate this to the wider world. Part of his 'youthful exuberance' came from the excitement of rediscovering his Yorkshire roots and, as early as 1956, he commented to the town's local paper that 'Huddersfield is a bright, attractive, progressive city' (qtd. in Ward 2013: 411).

Suddenly, interviews begin, not by describing a dour glower or a beating, but by referencing that 'he is a Northern lad' (Hall 1969) with the 'husk of [a] Yorkshire accent (Anon. 1967a) coming 'back to the mill' (Taylor 1969) to 'visit his parents [and make] 'a film that is good enough for Huddersfield' (Hibben 1969). His role as a self-educated, old-fashioned mill worker in the 1970 adaptation of Bill Naughton's play *Spring and Port Wine* consolidated Mason as 'of the North'. Although the film is set in Lancashire (not Yorkshire), his performance as the stubborn working-class patriarch drew reviews that admired the authenticity of his acting, with one commenting that 'a grizzled and grave James Mason ... surely draws a tap-root strength from the star's own Huddersfield background' (*Evening Standard* review, qtd. in Hirschhorn 1977: 207). He again used a broad local accent in his pantomime-style portrayal of the villainous Mr Grimes in *The Water Babies* (1978), desperate to escape the Victorian underclass and follow 'the promise of being a toff'. However, throughout these films, there is an anomalous interplay between the real and the enacted in Mason's identity. Whilst drawing on his regional upbringing to position himself as an 'authentic' part of Yorkshire heritage, as the son of a textile merchant schooled at Marlborough College and Cambridge University, Mason's background was not the self-contained working-class terraces of these films, yet he was convincingly placed in these spaces. Additionally, Mason's earlier sense of 'progressiveness' is rarely commuted into these screen images of him as a Northerner, despite the theme of the actor's 'rebecoming', as they rely heavily on the area's industrial heritage. This reclaiming of regional identity lies somewhere between 'youthfulness and modernity' and 'tradition and age', further adding to the paradoxical and conflicted nature of Mason's star persona.

The fervent screen engagement with his homeland culminated in a 1972 television programme Mason made for Yorkshire Television called *Home James*, where he takes us on a tour of Huddersfield.[15]

He narrates a picture of local character, performing an odd mix of roles: part-*flâneur*, part-anthropologist, part-local, part-visitor. As he guides the viewer through different local spaces, he defines Huddersfieldians as unique, tight, blunt and uncompromising. Although ostensibly a contemporaneous study of the town, the tone constantly represents Huddersfield as unchanged and untainted by time, a celebration of its present only through how closely it relates to its past. Whilst the film opens with the ex-native making an admittedly nostalgic journey to a place he no longer lives, Mason's commentary and the *mise en scène* constantly attempt to situate the star within the town, suggesting that James Mason *is* Huddersfield and Huddersfield *is* James Mason. However, it remains an odd balance between an objective and subjective text: in *isolation from*, but also *belonging to*. His description of the local character clearly mirrors qualities of Mason's star image, revealing that the belligerent attitude was not *his* alone, but that of his upbringing and surroundings. He aligns himself further, declaring, 'outsiders say *we* are tight', but then separates himself with descriptions of the locals as 'they' and distanced observations about 'how personal eccentricities are encouraged'. Mason is both 'of' and 'not of' the town.

In demonstrating the specific qualities of the townspeople (and Mason's contentious inclusion here), it is clear that the space is constructed as a unique one where the town stands alone and all inhabitants are equal. Class boundaries are exorcised in favour of a coherent local identity; Huddersfieldians 'belong together regardless of money or class'. Mason becomes emblematic of this: on screen, he constantly moves between class spaces and images, and changes in his costuming (smart tie and jacket, cloth cap and brown mac, and casual woollen turtleneck) make it difficult to locate a specific class identity in him. In the end, it is in the space of his own street – a location that concludes his tour – that best articulates his own sense of belonging. Walking along the street, he points down to the lower-class end and up to more affluent 'posh' houses, before gesturing to the location of his parents' house and striding off into their garden. The direction of the gesture and the editing of the sequence indicate that his home is in the middle of the street; a street that – in this romanticised utopian image of Huddersfield at least – is shown to be representative of the nature of the town itself and suggestive of why Mason felt nostalgic for it. Whereas his early British films construct an image of him as an aristocratic brute (at odds with the 'everyman' John Mills or the working-class Dirk Bogarde), the persona of the gruff, hard-working Yorkshireman hints at a more lower-class status, and here Mason references his actual middle-class origins. This suggests, that towards the end of his career, the transgressive qualities of his star image extended to class as well, despite the initial association with a fixed position of privilege in his star-making roles.

It is this relationship between inclusivity and identification, the past and present of Huddersfield and its people, and Mason himself that forms the focus of Paul Ward's examination of geographical/historical space and cultural identity, looking at positioning the attitudes of Huddersfield locals to Mason as a transatlantic film star. Despite the obviousness of the programme's utopian construction of the town and romanticised concept of 'belonging', Ward's charting of local oral history mirrors the image that *Home James* attempts to construct around the star. His interviews reveal a complex exchange between star and spectator that has been shaped by the regional identity, nostalgia and ageing of both parties. He concludes that through the pride in Mason as the 'local boy' who became a star and his reconnection with his home town, 'Mason prompted a sense of Yorkshireness in his audiences who saw him at the same time a Hollywood star, a romantic figure of desire *and* a citizen of Yorkshire and Huddersfield' (2014: 418), an identification made in spite of – or indeed enabled by – the many conflicting elements and identities that made up the star's persona. Ward writes that Mason identified as neither British nor American, and the star even commented himself that 'I might say the whole world is my home' (Anon. 1967b).

Throughout (and beyond) his life, Mason's persona embodied transgression, rebelliousness and tension but in a multitude of ways. This crucially includes transgressions between (and challenges to) that original romantically doomed and Byronically brutal image, negotiating between other identities of the ordinary and the excessive, domestic and eccentric, youth and tradition, cross-class, and whilst a figure *without nation*, one distinctly *with region*.

3 POWER

Interviewed just before his death, James Mason reflected back on his career: 'I don't think I have achieved what I set out to do. I wanted to have the power to be in command of my own career. I was never able to do so' (qtd. in Lewin 1983). The history of Mason is one of a man constantly attempting to use his star status as a means to gain independent control over his place in international systems of film production, railing against – what he saw as – restrictive contracts and lazy distribution networks, and a lack of industry ambition and funding. Running through accounts of the star's career is the belief that the power he wanted (and would ultimately measure his success by) would come from a freelance status and through the roles of writer, director and – most of all – producer. Mason recognised that the best way to achieve power in the film industry was to prove he was a sure-fire economic investment: 'I knew that if I became an international star I could make the money and have the reputation which would allow me to be my own boss and star in my own films' (qtd. in Bonner 1983). By the end of his life, his perceived failure to maintain an impressive star status meant that – to him – none of this was satisfactorily realised.

Ironically, given his goal of becoming a producer, Mason considered it his misfortune to be an actor during the heyday of the producer-led industries of British and Hollywood cinema, believing these systems left little space for the risk-taking of independent film production and a freelance economy. He was forward in voicing these concerns, firstly in his criticisms of the Rank Organisation in the 1940s, and in later attitudes towards monopoly organisation, Hollywood's production line operation, its burgeoning relationship with television and the American funding of international projects.[1] Actors' powers, he felt, were limited and locked into subservience by labour contracts and unchallenging film projects determined by the demands of a commercial marketplace. At times, these attempts to gain more control over his career backfired spectacularly, such as his public spat with Anthony Asquith, Rank and professional membership organisations over criticisms of the British film industry, and a lengthy breach-of-contract lawsuit in 1948 which temporarily prevented him from working in Hollywood. The expense of this lawsuit and his divorce in 1964 reportedly left him financially crippled: 'my farcical divorce cost me all I'd earned in my 15 or 16 years in the United States. I, James Mason ... was flat broke' (qtd. in Hirschhorn 1969).

However, whilst he may have felt powerless, it is clear that Mason's career was far from one of professional failure. He was able to make a number of critically acclaimed films that explored subjects intelligently and in which he delivered many much-admired performances, including (but certainly not limited to) *The Seventh Veil*, *Odd Man Out*, *The Reckless Moment*, *Bigger Than Life*, *A Star Is Born*, *Julius Caesar*, *North by Northwest*, *Lolita*, *The Verdict* and *The Shooting Party*. He had the opportunity to work with notable directors such as Alfred Hitchcock, Stanley Kubrick, Carol Reed, Michael Powell, Vincente Minnelli, Henry Hathaway, Robert Rossen, George Cukor, Joseph Mankiewicz, Sidney Lumet, Max Ophüls and Nicholas Ray. For the latter two, Mason's strong star power and contract stipulations were vital in ensuring the completion of the three films he made with them. He never entered into a long-term contract with any studio and many of his shorter contracts guaranteed large salaries, percentage profits, and the option of director, producer and writer roles. He had a benevolent association with Twentieth Century-Fox, including a solid relationship with its Head of Production Darryl Zanuck, as well as similarly positive encounters with the British producer Sydney Box. He also made a number of independent films, either with his own production companies, through his own financing arrangements, or with independent studios across Hollywood, Britain and Europe. To explore the theme of power that runs through Mason's life, this chapter will look at details from four key periods in his career to construct an economic reading of the star's work, contextualising it within wider film industry histories: Britain 1935–47, Hollywood 1949–51 and 1951–56, and Europe 1962–84. It begins, though, with a section on Mason's work as a writer, and how through this he uses 'power' as a mechanism of self-representation.

Mason as author

Perceptions of Mason's apparent powerlessness originate directly from the star himself: the articles he wrote for the British and American press, other interviews, his short commentaries in *The Films of James Mason* (Hirschhorn 1977) and *Before I Forget*, the autobiography published in 1981. Apart from the latter two end-of-career reflections, the majority of his writing was done in the late 1940s and early 1950s. This included letters to major publications, numerous invited columns for newspapers, articles for magazines such as *Lilliput*, *Cosmopolitan* and the *Pie* series, and John Monaghan's short biography – which was at least partly ghost-written by Mason.[2] That this was the time Mason was most vigorously trying to establish and then protect his star status (and come to terms with the supposed inevitability of contracted labour) is no coincidence. His self-penned publications recede from the late 1950s as his status and working environments fragment along with the film industries themselves.

Mason portrait photo

But in his later years, Mason remained consistently vocal about the industry, how it valued him and how it was developing financially and artistically, and – unusually – he openly discussed money, specifically how his lack of it shaped his film choices. It is obvious that writing was one of the ways Mason felt he could attain some sort of power over his career: articulating his frustrations with the industry and his place in it, demonstrating a progressive eye on what could change and documenting the conditions of his labour.

In these earlier articles, Mason positioned himself as a forward-thinking rebel, insistent on opposing established systems. He criticised, but also suggested creative solutions that he hoped might lead to superior products and an equality of power, yet retrospectively never saw himself as being able to implement any. As early as 1937 (whilst still a minor contract player), Mason wrote a letter to *Picture Show* magazine, making his argument clear: 'if we are to compete seriously with Hollywood we shall do so only by improving the standard of our cheap unpretentious films, forgetting our extravagant endeavours to capture the world market with super productions' (qtd. in Mason 1981: 130). In 1946, hot on the heels of the 'Yes, I beat my wife!' article, *Lilliput* magazine published 'I hate producers!', where Mason remonstrated that actors 'get the feeling that they aren't allowed to act. ... There is the constant demoralising presence of an assistant director whose only thought is to blow his whistle and start shooting' and considered the hierarchies of the British mode of film production an obstacle to decent performance, longing for the simplicity of the stage (1946a). This is indicative of a constant attitude of 'the grass is always greener' in Mason's world view, and his writings reveal an inconsistency in his evaluation of the industries he worked in – something not always clearly figured as an evolving perception coloured by maturity and experience. His 1946 farewell article 'Why I am going to America' cites the inefficiency of the Rank Organisation, and yet only a few years later (undated [but circa 1949]), he reflects negatively on the Hollywood studio system, writing, 'the British are far more efficient than the Americans [or rather] ... the efforts of the British are not hampered by a cumbersome and highly inefficient mechanism'. In between the two, he wrote a critical article for *Cosmopolitan* called 'Why I am afraid of going to Hollywood' (1948); the negative response to this helped forge his 'difficult' reputation that was enhanced by Louella Parsons's gossip broadcasts. All viewpoints are contested at some point in the pages of *Before I Forget*.

On publication, Mason's autobiography was criticised for lacking in anecdote and being 'politely unrevealing' (Macauley 2003), but it provides a detailed account of his working life, including contract negotiations, financial arrangements and reflections on the changing film industry. Throughout it, the author deliberately constructs himself as an individual constantly fighting to preserve professional dignity and market value, and to negotiate repressive systems of film production with which he felt at odds. In a passage as passionate as his earlier articles, on his experiences at Gainsborough Pictures, he writes, 'To me, producers were men who polluted the artistic aspirations of writers, directors and actors, who responded only to the promptings of vulgar men in Wardour Street' (1981: 186). More sedate but no less critical, on his work for MGM he reflects, 'None of us could deny that many films of high quality had been turned out by this factory but the more one heard about it the more disagreeable it sounded and more justification for thinking of it as a factory' (ibid.: 283). Then again, a few pages later, he looks back at Hollywood admiringly saying, 'Everything was so well organised in these factories that there was no audible griping. The producers may have been given a hard time by the studio bosses but they did not hand it on to the lower ranks' (ibid.: 308).

I will return to Mason's writing as a primary source throughout this chapter, as it provides the most consistently thorough account of his contractual history. But the quotes used above raise significant questions about the reliability of such self-authored material as a major source. Opinions about one's career and life can, of course, change over time – what is felt at thirty may not be a reflection shared at the age of seventy. But what strikes me about Mason's responses here and elsewhere is an underlying lack of awareness of the contradictions he makes, even in the same piece of writing. Wherever he is, he always seems to be in the worst position and vacillates between looking forward to new promises *elsewhere* (Hollywood in the late 1940s, Europe in the early 1960s) or back at better-but-now-lost opportunities (that he should have remained in the UK) that reveal a certain naivety about the reality of production industries. In 1961, he states that 'Hollywood's prestige has decreased as Europe's has risen. Now it is quite pointless to go to Hollywood' (qtd. in Mann), but by 1972 he commented, 'They say Spain and Italy are the new Hollywood ... I suppose they are all just about as awful as each other. One could spend one's life drifting around in international co-productions. I just don't much want to' (qtd. in Morley 1989: 157). His words remain part of the public discourse that configures him as the rebellious 'odd man out'. However, Mason could also play the star system as much as rebel against it, as illustrated by his apparent debunking of earlier statements about his first Hollywood film, *Caught* (1949):

People always ask why I chose to start my Hollywood career with *Caught*. I used to make up some important-sounding reason, like having to work with Ophüls or being fascinated by the script. The truth of the matter was that I was desperately broke [and] needed a job. (Qtd. in ibid.: 84)

The degree to which either position is 'the whole truth' remains open; what is important here is how Mason uses the incident to create and then diminish a sense of his own power and control during various stages of his career. So I acknowledge the subjective positions within Mason's writing and am certainly wary of using his words as 'truths' – beyond the basic terms of contracts, contacts and salaries, their value is in their representational qualities. His authored pieces also convey an inherently insular nature to his evaluations: his power (or lack of it) as an *individual*, and, even though he remonstrates against whole industries, the locus by which he identifies problems and solutions is always himself alone. But – to take the most significant challenge to this – Mason entered Hollywood at a time of immense flux where, following the Paramount decrees in 1948, the industry underwent huge changes to its whole system of operation. Contextualising the labour history of Mason enables a move beyond the individual, to situate his viewpoints more objectively within a bigger picture of national and transnational cinemas, industrial and employment structures, economic developments and the labour management of other artists, where the instability of his career can be considered in light of these factors.

Britain 1935–47

Mason pitted his career as a labour battle between himself, Britain and Hollywood. However, even his first years on screen relied heavily on the transnational nature of the film industry in the 1930s and benefited from the close relationship between the two national industries. In 1935 (after an abortive attempt to work on Alexander Korda's *The Private Life of Don Juan*), Mason met the American Al Parker, who would become the star's agent and long-time manager, but was at that time running the British branch of Fox Film Corporation (later Twentieth Century-Fox). The creation of British subsidiary companies by Hollywood studios was typical of the era, being a way to negotiate the UK Cinematograph Films Act of 1927 that required the production and exhibition of a quota of British films. Hollywood targeted the UK and other large European markets, commissioning and funding low-budget filmmaking across the continent.[3] Mason's first screen roles were in American-produced quota-quickies for Fox Films UK directed by Parker: *Late Extra*, *Blind Man's Bluff* (1936) and *Troubled Waters* (1936).[4] He was soon on the radar of Hollywood, signing a contract with Fox that offered a competitive salary (far above his earnings in the theatre) and guaranteed annual increments, and he also signed with the American talent agency run by Myron Selznick (brother of David). But almost immediately, Mason found the contract arrangement limiting, as he had to fight to persuade Fox to agree to a loan-out so he could participate in the big-budget production of *The Mill on the Floss*. The battle temporarily soured his relationship with Parker until 1939, and the studio did not renew his contract, preferring to entice other contract stars (including George Sanders) to California (Morley 1989: 41). Mason followed this experience with his first scathing review of the British film industry in *Picture Show*.

Disillusioned with the system, Mason created his own independent production company with Pamela and Roy Kellino, whom he had met on the set of *Troubled Waters*. Over the next two years, the three of them wrote, acted in, produced and directed the low-budget feature *I Met a Murderer*. This was the first of a number of films that the Masons had close control over; they wrote, produced and starred together in the UK production of *The Upturned Glass*, co-produced with Sydney Box. Pamela and Mason also made US productions *Charade*, *Lady Possessed* (1952) and *The Child*. Along with Mason's involvement as producer on the studio-produced films *Bigger Than Life*, *Hero's Island* (1962) and *Age of Consent*, these examples show that he maintained a periodic level of production authority throughout his career. However, few of these projects were commercial or critical successes (and none were both). *I Met a Murderer* also brought Mason into conflict with Gaumont-British Film Corporation. Gaumont was run by the Ostrer brothers, including Pamela's father, Isidore. The Masons took the film to Gaumont hoping for a family-favoured distribution deal; this was refused, and, according to Mason, Gaumont discouraged other companies from making an alternative deal with them (1981: 149). This slight 'left Mason with a residual loathing for the British film distribution network which was to erupt a few years later into a long and damaging battle with the Rank Organisation' (Morley 1989: 46). Although Mason located his diminished control exclusively in terms of a 'national' cinema, the Ostrers had close ties with Hollywood through a financial arrangement with Fox Film Corporation, continuing the transnational nature of British cinema (Murphy 1996: 53). Mason also later made a profit of £20,000 on the film through an American distribution deal for cinema and television (Anon. 1975).

Under the Ostrers, Gaumont-British Corporation had absorbed Gainsborough Pictures during the 1940s, and was in turn then taken over by the Rank Organisation, so Mason engaged in power plays with all three at the height of his British popularity. In 1943, Gainsborough pursued Mason for *The Man in Grey* and a multiple-picture contract. Initially reluctant, he was persuaded of the film's commercial potential by Al Parker and to accept the contract for five films. Mason's slim control seemed to plummet almost overnight: now a highly valuable commercial product marketed as 'the man you love to hate',

> he hated being at the beck and call of any producer or director for more than about ten weeks, let alone enslaved for months, if not years to a studio, still largely run by the hated in-laws who had been so unhelpful over *I Met a Murderer*. (Morley 1989: 56)

But there were significant respites from this. He was able to negotiate completion of non-studio films he had committed to prior to the contract, and, according to co-star Stewart Granger, negotiated a salary well above the other Gainsborough stars (qtd. in ibid.: 57). A clause was also inserted into his contract for *The Wicked Lady*, stipulating that none of Mason's scenes could be cut without his approval, and despite loathing the film he made sure to keep his screen time intact (Mason 1981: 187).

The most public rebellion against Gainsborough was through his articles in the British press critiquing filmmaking practice ('Glamour' and 'I hate producers!'), which raised the ire of the Association of Cine-Technicians (and their president, Anthony Asquith[5]) and the British Film Producers' Association. In 1946, Mason extended his public complaints towards J. Arthur Rank, owner of the Rank Organisation – and by default, Gainsborough and Gaumont. In interviews with the *Daily Express* and *Life* magazine, he expressed concern at Rank's increasingly monopolistic power over the film industry, that his background as a businessman who made his money in the flour-milling trade meant that Rank knew a lot about flour but nothing about cinema, and that he treated Mason solely as a commercial product no different from worsteds or branded synthetic flour (Anon. 1946; Osborne 1947: 38). Later, Mason reconstructed this attack as a desire to merely 'annoy' his British employers as he left the lacklustre industry for the excitement of Hollywood (1981: 210). He also suggested that his initial reception in the US as 'uncooperative' was managed by American-based Rank publicists feeding negative stories to Louella Parsons. However, there were accusations that this public attack by the UK's biggest star was down to family loyalty to the Ostrers, as Rank's takeover of Gaumont had diminished their control of the studio. Head of Production Maurice Ostrer (Pamela's uncle) shared Mason's views that Rank was a weak mogul who engaged in ineffective production organisation, and discontented with the bureaucracy of the Rank Organisation, Maurice had resigned in 1946.[6] In a letter to Hedda Hopper (1946c), Mason refuted the claims that his anti-Rank feelings came from personal circumstances, claiming that they were based on a singular frustration with the British film industry, but this is compromised by his insistence that the Ostrers themselves 'root for Rank', considering the evidence to the contrary.

Mason's difficult attitude and public condemnation of Rank led to his contract being dissolved before the completion of his fifth contracted film. Returning to freelance status, he described his pleasure at being able to turn down unsuitable roles to pursue more opportune experiences such as independent work with Sydney Box. Mason recognised a kindred spirit in the producer, and together they completed *The Seventh Veil* and *The Upturned Glass*, the former being developed by Box and co-written with his wife, Muriel. When Mason became available (having turned down *I Know Where I'm Going!* [1945]), Box saw an opportunity to exploit the power of Mason's cruel-but-attractive star image, as it would ensure a West End premiere and extensive distribution, even if it added a £10,000 salary to the film's medium-sized budget (Spicer 2006: 53). Mason also had the power to insist on script revisions that enhanced his role as Nicholas (to be written by Pamela) (ibid.). Charles Drazin writes that,

Mason would have been drawn to Box as an individual risking his own money, rather than an executive implementation of the production programme of a faceless corporation ... [and had] his opinions respected and [was] made to feel part of a rewarding creative process. (2007: 207)

However, despite this utopic vision of independence, *The Seventh Veil* and its box-office success relied heavily on the Rank Organisation. After the project had been rejected by Columbia Pictures, Box approached Rank for funding and the mogul agreed a finance and distribution deal, guaranteeing £75,000 of the costs and ensuring widespread release in the UK and the US through the company's national and international distribution and exhibition circuits (Spicer 2006: 51). Nevertheless, the association with Box proved to be a financially rewarding one and *The Seventh Veil* was a huge international success. Mason then made *The Upturned Glass*, although 'this was very much Mason's project than Box's', who handed over the producer role to the star and to his sister, Betty Box (ibid.: 71). At the same time, Box took over Maurice Ostrer's role as managing director of the Rank Organisation in 1946. Later, on Mason's arrival in the United States, Al Parker rumoured the star's salary for *The Upturned Glass* to be $240,000 plus percentages (which he estimated to total $160,000), most likely in a strategy to help raise Mason's going rate to a competitive Hollywood level (Osborne 1947: 40).

The same year as *The Seventh Veil*, Hollywood studios again expressed serious interest in the star. Having been contracted to Fox ten years earlier, Mason met with Spyros Skouras, the head of parent company Twentieth Century-Fox, to discuss a move to California; however, as the proposed deal was for a long-term contract, the star declined it (Mason 1981: 203). Throughout the 1940s, Paramount Pictures had also been keen to sign the star, and David Rose, the head of the studio's British outfit, met with him frequently. Initially resistant, in 1946 Mason, anxious to make full use of his new freelance status and leave behind a UK industry now in recession, began talks. By then, Rose reported (perhaps erroneously) that Paramount was

The Seventh Veil (1945)

no longer interested but that he – tired of the system – had left the company to start as a talent agent and producer. Rose proposed an independent partnership with Mason where their choice of films would be funded with Hollywood money: '[Rose] would take care of the finance, I the artistic side … No run of the mill contract for me' (ibid.: 219). Driven by the desire for control, and buoyed by the rewarding experience with Box (although ignoring Rank's role in this), Mason jumped at the chance of an offer of a Hollywood-based independent career.

The arrangement turned out to be the biggest fiasco of his career. To entice major Hollywood interest, on Rose's request Mason wrote a letter outlining their intention to form a business partnership, but Rose's Hollywood negotiations proved inadequate for the star, as the producer pursued deals with minor studios like Universal or independent ones aligned with Eagle Lion, Rank's US distribution subsidiary. After Rose attempted once more to align the star with Paramount with the offer of a ten-picture contract where 'no actor at Paramount is guaranteed the same freedom and personal authority as I have got for you' [Mason 1981: 223], but with no options for a production role), Mason cut his ties with the agent/producer, making his own path to America, where – on arrival – he was approached by Alexander Korda, who offered him a six-picture deal and an advance of £50,000.[7] Rose then claimed that Mason's letter constituted a legal contract and launched a breach-of-contract lawsuit demanding that Mason either settle for $1million or be prevented from working with another producer for two years. Stubborn at having lost control of a situation, Mason, 'acting on a point of principle' and loath to give Rose part of his salary for two years, refused to settle out of court (ibid.: 237). Although, in the end, Mason won the court case, it took two years and cost £100,000. During this time he was unable to work on any films and failed to capitalise on the contract with Korda, on Hollywood interest from Samuel Goldwyn, RKO and others, and on the US success of his British films. Compromised by his bid to become an independent Hollywood producer even before he reached California and disillusioned by the system that Rose had come from, it was only in 1949 that he started his Hollywood career.

Hollywood 1949–51

That Mason was a rebel who challenged a repressive system prevails throughout stories of his time in Hollywood, continuing the defiant attitude that characterised his involvement with the British studio system and consolidation as the perennial 'odd man out'. There is an underlying narrative that Mason's uncompromising nature and refusal to conform to established systems of business and production precipitated his downfall as a viable Hollywood star player. A 1954 telegram communication between Mason and Warner Bros. chief,

Jack Warner, does illustrate the star's inherent rebellious streak. Nearing the release of the Warner Bros.-produced *A Star Is Born*, Warner learned that Mason would not be attending the premiere nor the following celebration at the Coconut Grove. Seeing this as a failure to perform appropriate promotional duties, he cabled the star requesting his appearance:

There's an old adage one must put something back if they want to continue taking something out. Assure you only good can come from your attending. Affair will be covered by hundreds of radio and television stations throughout USA and world, so why not get on the team? (Warner 1954)

Mason declined the invitation, unwilling to 'put in' in order to 'take out'. If he was going to succeed, it would be on his terms alone.

The view painted of Hollywood by Mason and others is of an unshakeable monolithic structure in full control of star labour. Olga Franklin's 1953 portrait describes 'how he hissed at Hollywood!' (1953), and in 1983, an article announces 'that [Mason] never quite made it, because he bucked the studio star processing system which even dictated who your friends were' (Bonner). Morley notes that whilst Mason's unwillingness to sign a studio contract or compromise his artistic integrity is now typical, 'in 1948, it was regarded as the policy of a dangerously anti-studio foreign rebel' (1989: 83). However, this is a romanticised view of the outsider artist fighting a battle against the Hollywood Goliath, with little grounding in economic reality, and was predominantly circulated in Britain, where the cultural value of a home-grown star 'cocking a snook' at America would have been a popular one. (It is also indicative of the rather confused and contradictory relationship between Mason and the British press.)

Mason's arrival in 1948 coincided, not with a secure studio system but with the Paramount decrees, which destabilised the whole industry through the legal ruling that found the vertical integration and oligopolistic control of the major studios illegal and, in the years that followed, mandated a divesture of studio-owned theatres and release of contracted players, increasing opportunities for production and distribution deals between independent companies and the established studios. It was also a time of falling audiences, an industry-wide decrease in film production and the rise of television, all of which hastened the end of the so-called Golden Age of the Hollywood studio system. Denise Mann (2008) characterises the changing environment of the Hollywood post-1948 era as one which ultimately provided greater autonomy to creative personnel who capitalised on the instability of the industry and maintained greater control of their careers throughout freelance and producer roles. Nonexclusive freelance contracts became the norm: in 1944, 804 actors were under contract to the major studios, but this fell to 164 in 1961, commensurate with new studio preferences of bidding on talent in the open market (Carman and Drake 2015: 217). The dismantling of the studios' in-house producer-led system meant the rise of the 'package system', where leading talent agencies like the William Morris Agency prospered by developing whole projects tied to the employment of their A-list clientele on short-term or freelance contracts (including percentage deals).[8] These deals prefigured the New Hollywood system of the 1960s and beyond and the modern characterisation of the relationship between talent and studio as one of 'dependent independence' (McDonald 2013: 166). Tom Kemper's (2010) and Emily Carman's (2016) histories of talent agencies and independent stardom demonstrate how the rise of both agent and freelance star can be traced back to Hollywood of the 1930s, well before the break-up of the studio system. Carman highlights that whilst Hollywood histories have always acknowledged individual case studies of stars' struggles to escape confining studio contracts, such as James Cagney, Olivia de Havilland and Bette Davis, these have been presented as 'flashpoints' of exceptional circumstances. Instead, freelance contracts and percentage deals were more common in Hollywood A-list stardom than this and talent agents were already brokering deals for many major female stars as early as 1931. In this context, Mason was neither rebel nor outsider to the industry that sought to employ him in the 1950s. He, as many others did, benefited from an unstable industry that was having to experiment with the organisation of individual and corporate power in order to remain an economic powerhouse.

On his arrival in Hollywood, Mason signed with the William Morris talent agency under agent Abe Lastfogel. Lastfogel's first plan was to offer Mason to MGM on a long-term contract, which he immediately rejected, but it was obvious that despite his enforced absence from production, the star still had commercial value in the eyes of the major studios. Mason often explained his apparently lacklustre Hollywood career through the failure of his first five films, which took him years to recover from economically (Mason 1981: 277). Four of these films were made in 1949: *Caught*, *Madame Bovary*, *The Reckless Moment* and *East Side, West Side*. *One Way Street* followed the year after. Two of the films were produced by MGM (*Bovary* and *East Side*). Given his initial rejection of Lastfogel's deal with MGM, it might be assumed that Mason was then forced to sign a three-film deal with them, relinquishing the freelance status he longed for. However, all were negotiated on a film-by-film basis with an agreed salary payment. The other three films had similar terms, two of which were produced by independent companies (*Caught* for Enterprise and *The Reckless Moment* for Walter Wanger), whilst *One Way Street* was made for the 'Little Three' studio Universal.[9] The film that followed (and Mason's first commercial success), *Pandora and the Flying Dutchman*, was written, produced and directed by Albert Lewin, who was contracted to MGM, with an additional arrangement to make independently produced films if he offered MGM first refusal for distribution. *Pandora* was therefore made by Lewin's newly formed production company Romulus Films and distributed by MGM. Both the contracts for *Pandora* and *Caught* guaranteed Mason a percentage of each film's profits.

So what does this reveal? In his first five films, Mason worked extensively with independent producers and on a freelance basis. He was paid well and with a steady increment in salary demands, monitored closely in the press. This results in some inconsistencies in the amounts paid (not least because UK sources quote pounds sterling and US sources quote dollars), but gives a sense of rising economic value that was consolidated beyond 1951. For *Caught*, he earned £37,000 plus percentages (approx. $50,000). For his ten days' work on *Madam Bovary*, his salary was reported anywhere in between £3,750 per day (all BFI clippings file), £20,000 in total (Morley 1989: 87), $50,000 for *three* days and $125,000 *per week* (both Hirschberg 1949). Hirschberg's article stated that in 1949, Mason's rate was $150,000 plus 25 per cent of the profits, although this seems likely to be an exaggeration given his salary for *Caught* and records of his rate in the mid-1950s, with a British article quoting his price in 1952 at £50,000 per film (Gourlay 1952). These figures support the reports that he was being paid between five and ten times his British rate (£10,000 for *The Seventh Veil*). Although one cannot be precise about his wages, it would seem believable that in 1949 Mason probably earned around $200,000 between his four films. To put this into context, this locates him in the bracket of the mid-range star – for comparison, the similarly mid-range star Dana Andrews, who was under contract with Twentieth Century-Fox, earned an annual salary of $155,000 for 1948 and $215,000 for 1949 (Rollyson 2012: 200), whilst in 1948, the higher-level star Barbara Stanwyck brokered a salary of $125,000 in an independently contracted one-picture deal for *Sorry, Wrong Number* (Carman 2016: 161) (one of the two films she made that year),[10] and James Stewart's going rate per picture in 1949 was $200,000.

It is revealing to look further at Mason's first project, *Caught*. Mason describes that his involvement came through realising that his stipulation of no long-term contracts had cut him off from the major studios, forcing him to look to below-the-line independent producers. The most noteworthy of these, Samuel Goldwyn, already had 'giant freelance actors like Ronald Colman and Gary Cooper … to satisfy his requirements', so Mason was left with the 'small fry' (Mason 1981: 269). He considered working for Enterprise Studios, who made *Caught*, as a compromise of his star status and power. Enterprise Studios had been founded in 1946 by David L. Loew, Charles Einfeld and A. Pam Blumenthal, and then amalgamated with the actor John Garfield's production company Roberts Productions once Garfield's Warner Bros. contract expired. Like Mason, Garfield wished to remain a freelance artist with creative control over his projects and to enable other artists the same freedom. Between 1947 and 1949, Enterprise made nine films, most famously *Body and Soul* (1947) and *Force of Evil* (1948), starring Garfield and directed by Abraham Polonsky. *Body and Soul* was a major commercial success and the studio seemed to have a promising future. As Brian Neve notes, the studio attracted radical and liberal artists, citing director Robert Aldrich's description of it as 'embodying a communal way to make films', where 'there was nobody at the head of the studio to bring us all up short' (1992: 126). Denise Mann calls Enterprise 'perhaps the greatest of all Hollywood anomalies', where revolving credit, leased studio space and a distribution agreement with United Artists and then MGM offered the chance for left-inclined talent to make challenging films and participate in the profits (2008: 71–72).

Caught was directed by the noted German-born (French-based) Jewish director Max Ophüls, who had been in exile in Hollywood since 1941. In 1948, he had directed *Letter from an Unknown Woman*, which (as with his films with Mason) was not a success on release, but has since become critically acclaimed. Marked by failed Hollywood projects, Ophüls returned to France in 1950. *Caught* is the story of the upwardly mobile Leonora Eames (Barbara Bel Geddes) who marries the sadistic multimillionaire Smith Ohlrig (Robert Ryan). Realising her predicament, she flees and finds work with the tough but dedicated Dr Quinada (Mason). Slowly she and Quinada fall in love, although unbeknownst to him, Leonora is pregnant by Ohlrig.

Caught (1949)

Despite Mason's reservations about Enterprise, the studio and project seemed in line with his wider filmmaking ambitions. Ophüls had approached Enterprise with an early treatment of *Caught* and although the pre-production stage was fraught with difficulties, Mason was keen to work with the director, and Enterprise were keen to sign the star. When he did, 'Einfeld and Loew considered it a coup. Getting the British star was certainly worth doubling the budget for his part to $150,000 plus a percentage of the profits' (Bacher 1996: 214). Bacher notes that Enterprise's filmmaking policy relied on securing a singular star presence and that the studio saw Mason as such an investment. It was an arrangement agreeable to both, as Mason saw the film as a way of avoiding typecasting as a villain – although initially approached for Ohlrig, he insisted that Abe Lastfogel negotiate a deal where he could play the more sympathetic Quinada.

The film tested positively but failed on wider release. Mason attributed the lack of success to compromises in artistic integrity: interference from the executive producers Einfeld and Loew in Ophüls' methodical visual techniques and from the Production Code Administration over its contentious subject matter (Mason 1981: 271–72). But there was more going on here. *Body and Soul* had been Enterprise's only financial success and the company had been struggling throughout its whole operation, relying too heavily on a system that could only generate profits on a film-by-film basis. Their strategy had been to enter into a series of swiftly produced films that would be distributed by MGM. Loew and Einfeld's increased presence was to ensure the film was delivered quickly and on budget to try and recoup some of the studio's mounting losses. As Bacher describes, 'As the studio's financial position deteriorated, [Wolfgang Reinhardt, the producer] would continue to be caught between Ophüls' demands and the studio's declining ability to satisfy them. But those were matters of execution, not contests over artistic control' (1996: 227). The initial aims of the independent studio of implementing new modes of organisational and economic procedure were not sustainable and the company went into liquidation after the film's completion. Therefore, *Caught* became the culmination of a series of failures by an unstable studio rather than a singular flop. As Mann describes, '[Enterprise's] grand experiment in creating a platform for leftist filmmakers committed the cardinal Hollywood sin: failure to satisfy the bottom line of profits', also noting that its days would have been numbered anyway with the rise of HUAC and the impending blacklist (2008: 72).

However, Mason did not similarly suffer and despite *Caught*'s box-office failure, he was still considered a significant star. Following *Madame Bovary*,[11] he worked again with Ophüls on another semi-independent production, *The Reckless Moment*, produced by Walter Wanger and starring Wanger's wife, Joan Bennett. The film was financed and distributed by Columbia Pictures, who retained some control over the project, which fitted into their post-war economic strategy of fewer films of higher quality. As Bacher outlines, having 'recently scaled back its serials and B-production in favour of more A-production, a low-budget, A-film featuring a strong star like Mason ... was an attractive proposition' (1996: 265–66). Abe Lastfogel again negotiated a contract that included a level of artistic control whereby Mason had final director approval. Although his first choice – Jean Renoir – proved too expensive, he was happy to return to Ophüls as a replacement. Having developed his role as an independent producer throughout the 1940s, Wanger is categorised by Denise Mann alongside Walt Disney, Samuel Goldwyn and David O. Selznick as the most established of this breed (2008: 68); so, after his reservations about Enterprise Studios, Mason soon progressed to working with the high-level independent producers that he originally wanted. While working on *The Reckless Moment*, he also established a close friendship with Wanger and Joan Bennett.[12] Like Mason, Bennett had also wanted to gain greater control over her career. Her sister Constance Bennett had been a pioneer of independent stardom in the 1930s (Carman 2016), and in the mid-1940s Joan set up her own company, Diana Productions, with Wanger and Fritz Lang, making the films noirs *The Woman in the Window* (1944), *Scarlet Street* (1945) and *Secret Beyond the Door* (1948). What is particularly significant here (especially considering their friendship) is that Bennett's move into freelance production undercuts Mason's representation of himself as a somewhat lone figure of rebellion who – with hindsight – concluded that this insistence on control could not succeed in such an age and industry.

Hollywood 1951–56

In 1951, Mason began an association with Twentieth Century-Fox that lasted until the end of the decade. Unlike Enterprise Studios' ineffective leadership, Fox had the strong, autocratic leader in Head of Production Darryl Zanuck, who set a clear agenda about the types of films to be made and the implementation of studio policy and management. Following *Pandora*, Mason was approached by the studio to play Field Marshal Rommel in *The Desert Fox*. Telling the story of a leading Nazi figure from a sympathetic perspective, it was a controversial picture but in line with the production strategy begun by Zanuck in the 1940s of high-quality drama. Mason was keen to secure the role even though it meant he had to sign his first extended contract agreement: 'only for two years and I had a certain say in the selection of parts ... I was allowed to reject the first two parts they offered me but I was obliged to accept the third' (Mason 1981: 300).

There are some inconsistencies in the contract terms beyond this: Morley records that Mason was offered the contract only after the success of *The Desert Fox* (1989: 93), whilst a 1953 article mentions that it included options to write and direct. What none of them note is that it did not tie Mason exclusively to the studio, and he worked extensively on a freelance basis for other major and independent studios for the duration of the contract. For Fox he then made *Five Fingers* (1952), a cameo in the sequel to *The Desert Fox*, *The Desert Rats* (1953), and *Prince Valiant* (1954). He also worked on films produced and distributed by major studios – for MGM, *The Prisoner of Zenda* (1952), *The Story of Three Loves* (1953) and *Julius Caesar*; for Paramount, *Botany Bay* (1953); and for Warner Brothers, *A Star Is Born*. Three projects were made for independent studios and/or with minor studio distribution: *20,000 Leagues under the Sea* (1954) for Disney; *Face to Face* (1952) for Huntingdon Hartford/RKO; and again with Carol Reed on *The Man Between* for British Lion/United Artists. He also made two independent projects as actor, producer and writer (with Pamela and Roy Kellino): *Lady Possessed* and *Charade*. These years also saw a consistency in Mason's asking price: the Fox contract would earn him £150,000 for the three films (Franklin 1953) and he was paid £250,000 for both *A Star Is Born* and *20,000 Leagues under the Sea*. For the latter film, Mason would receive 10 per cent of gross receipts up to $125,000, and he was paid the full amount in 1956 (Anon. 1956).

The first of his films for Fox, *Five Fingers*, was conceived by director Joseph Mankiewicz to fulfil the final terms of his own contract with Fox and was designed to appeal to Zanuck's propensity for successful semi-documentary dramas. Based on a true story, it is a wartime spy thriller about a valet to the British ambassador in Ankara who is an Axis spy – code name 'Cicero' (Mason). Mason plays Cicero with a bitter wit, emphasising how his ostensive subordinate status enables the exchange of information and the motivations of this Machiavellian character. *Five Fingers* was initially a realistic war drama, but Mankiewicz rewrote parts of the script to emphasise noirish elements of betrayal, class distinctions and human frailty (Bray Lower and Barton Palmer 2001: 62–63), whilst Zanuck was heavily involved in the production and final edit. The film was a financial success, and although the director–producer collaboration was a fruitful one, with Mankiewicz commenting, 'I was very happy at Twentieth Century-Fox, and I can't think of another studio I ever felt that way about' (qtd. in Behlmer 1993: xix), he also resented the extent of Zanuck's control over the editing of his films and on release from his contract in 1953 formed his own production company, Figaro Inc. Denise Mann explores how the dynamics of the Zanuck–Mankiewicz relationship and their struggle for artistic power reflects the larger industrial and cinematic developments of the era: of the rise of the studio-based auteur, the balance between commercial and high-cultural projects, and slow shift into the New Hollywood system of financing and distribution (2008: 123–43), and Mason's work with both of them should also be considered in this context. Free from his Fox contract, Mankiewicz also worked in and out of the studio system and he directed Mason in their next film, *Julius Caesar*, for MGM, another critical and commercial success that mixed traditions of the Shakespearean stage with contemporary elements in its diverse casting of Mason, John Gielgud and Marlon Brando.

Five Fingers (1952)

The star recalls how Mankiewicz's creative control and individual style suffered under the weight of the 'studio machinery' (Mason 1981: 309), and the director's next few projects were independently produced, including *The Barefoot Contessa* (1954) and *The Quiet American* (1958), where in both he wanted to cast Mason in significant semi-leading roles. However, Mason rejected them, explaining the first rejection explicitly in terms of a perceived lack of 'power': 'I was not getting anywhere fast. The first step towards the acquisition of power to control my own destiny was to win enormous popularity by putting on the macho image with which the male ticket buyer would wish to identify with' (ibid.: 325). He felt that the proposed role of – in his words – an impotent Italian count could not achieve this, especially as Humphrey Bogart had secured the film's 'macho' role. Mankiewicz and Mason's relationship became characterised by a series of power plays; each tried to get the other involved in subsequent projects, although ultimately to no avail, as either their independent freelance status proved too financially risky or their schedules could not be reconciled. Despite writing in 1955 of being 'anxious to refresh [our] acquaintance' and in 1956 just coming off the studio flop *Bigger Than Life*, Mason, unwilling to film on location in Indochina, rejected *The Quiet American*. In 1957, the star sent repeated communications to Figaro Inc. about producing further films based on *Five Fingers*, which were met with only polite disinterest – apparently based on Mason's decreased star value.[13] Ten years later, on Mankiewicz's request for him to star in a play he had written and was to direct in New York, Mason declared himself 'wilfully unavailable' to appear in plays, as he preferred to keep himself open to film offers.[14]

During the mid-1950s, Mason left the William Morris Agency and signed with the Charlie Feldman Agency.[15] Tom Kemper's history of the rise of Hollywood agencies discusses Charlie Feldman at length, characterising him as an innovative practitioner in the art of contract negotiation. From the 1930s onwards, Feldman was instrumental in the history of Hollywood power and political economy by pioneering freelance, non-exclusive contracts, brokering package deals and ensuring percentage profits as standard. Kemper notes how Feldman's relationship with the studios was inherently non-combative and that he formed a long-time friendship with many of the major moguls, including Zanuck. As such, Feldman offers 'an alternative perspective in the so-called golden age of Hollywood, illustrating numerous exceptions to this era's adherence to the ironclad option contract' (2010: 74–75). And in the 1950s, Mason occupied a creative and economic space that allowed him to benefit from these innovations and associations.

Mason, Zanuck and Feldman collided – at least at the pre-production stage – on *Bigger Than Life*, and the film's development can be seen as the culmination of each of their respective ethoses. Feldman developed the project initially; whilst renegotiating Mason's short-term contract, Feldman offered Zanuck a deal to hire the star as an actor with options as a producer, writer and director. Zanuck

Bigger Than Life (1956)

agreed and Mason finally achieved the Hollywood power he desired, recalling the pleasure with which he informed members of the Fox executive network that he was now a 'staff producer' (Mason 1981: 375–77). Questioning Zanuck's new generosity regarding the distribution of power, Mason places this in the context of a changing industry, the Head of Production's tiring of the studio environment and his friendship with Feldman. In 1956, Zanuck left Fox to become a Paris-based independent producer, maintaining a distribution deal through Fox. Mason notes that,

before he launched his new career, [Zanuck] made some generous deals with old friends in Hollywood to keep them happy during his absence. Charlie was a great one for buying the rights of plays and books and ... developing these as film projects. Zanuck bought about a dozen of these for an impressive sum. I, being a client of Charlie's, also benefitted. (Ibid.: 373)

Bigger Than Life originated from an article by Berton Roueché in *The New Yorker* entitled 'Ten Feet Tall' about the devastating side effects of the drug cortisone. Mason played the small-town schoolteacher Ed Avery, who physically and mentally crumbles under the pressure of his suburbanite consumerist family life. Told he has only a few months to live, he begins a revolutionary treatment of cortisone, but this leads to an increasingly violent psychosis directed at his wife, Lou (Barbara Rush), and son, Richie (Christopher Olsen).

Mason was given the go-ahead by Zanuck's replacement, Buddy Adler, and with control over writer and director, the star-turned-producer shaped it into a cohesive project. Although previously associated with trends in cinematic realism and black-and-white photography, prior to his departure Zanuck had adopted other technological developments which now dominated Fox's output (following wider developments across the industry), and this strategy continued under Adler. Therefore, *Bigger Than Life* was made in Fox's trademarked widescreen format, Cinemascope, and filmed in

Eastman's colour process, Deluxe; and as a result, Mason opted for Nicholas Ray to direct, as he had been impressed by Ray's use of widescreen and colour in *Rebel Without a Cause* a year earlier.

Mason took on the role of hands-on producer with relish. In addition to Ray, he interviewed writers for the project (hiring Cyril Hume and Richard Maibaum), co-ordinated the relevant studio departments and liaised with the Production Code Administration. As a result, Mason occupied a new space within the filmmaking process and experienced a very different form of power relations. For all his previous criticisms, he followed the traditional studio routine of production practice, whereby 'only when the staff producer [Mason] had developed a script to the satisfaction of himself and the studio boss [would] a director [be] approached' (Mason 1981: 380). But this space was one of the 'middle-ground'. He was still below the studio boss and the demands of dominant studio practice; he recognised but also loathed the necessary use of Cinemascope and Deluxe, wishing he 'had the weight' to persuade Adler to allow the use of black and white. He also negotiated between the authorities and the director – to some degree powerless between the two. On this film, Mason was no longer the 'rebel' – this status belonged to Ray. Peter Biskind describes how Ray adopted and presented an 'independent rebellious stance' even at this time, which was evident on Mason's project (1974: 32). Firstly, Ray insisted on hiring the British journalist Gavin Lambert as a 'dialogue director' and Lambert made extensive script rewrites, as did Mason himself (Lambert 1958: 27). Ray then suggested bringing in the playwright Clifford Odets to help further, but Mason rejected this and was supported by Adler when Ray tried to go above his producer's head. But Ray sneaked Odets in regardless to rewrite new scenes that were submitted for filming without full approval, and in the end Mason-the-executive capitulated to Odets' involvement, even defending the move when challenged by other executives (Mason 1981: 382–87). Throughout the project, the star-producer seemed to be in control of very little – neither boss nor rebel, but mediator.

On its release in 1956, *Bigger Than Life* was a commercial and critical disaster, with Sheridan Morley describing it as 'killing off almost all the dreams James had left of a career behind the camera, or one which would allow him to control his own destiny as an actor' (1989: 116).[16] Mason cited three main reasons for its failure: the controversial subject matter, the colour and Cinemascope, which detracted from its credibility, and his own casting, whereby his 'foreign' status prevented the average American audience from identifying with his character (Mason 1981: 380). And yet, these 'failed' elements are key reasons which later led to the film's reappraisal (in addition to a refocus as a result of Ray's own rising auteur status amongst critics). Amy Lawrence notes how the psychic pain of Mason's character is displaced onto his body and house, where Ray's studied *mise en scène* uses widescreen to emphasise architectural structure, creating bisected and confining narrow spaces – from staircases to kitchens – that convey the critique of the American suburban life, and that the horizontal framing of the hospitalised Ed constructs his body as an abstracted subject (2010: 101–02). Expressionistic lighting creates dark shadows as Ed's behaviour becomes more monstrous, and as he comes to dominate so fully and aggressively, the colour fades from the overall aesthetic, beginning with vibrant yellows and reds before beige and finally darkest grey take over. Mason's 'foreignness' is also more complex than his dismissal here. Throughout his Hollywood career Mason's image negotiated elements of the ordinary, the intellectual and the exotic, and he was never wholly the 'foreign other' that he presents himself as in his critique. Whilst Amy Lawrence does characterise Mason as 'never easy to envision as ordinary' (ibid.: 100), Sam Wasson emphasises how the film builds on the way his performance changes from one of identifiable 'ordinariness' and 'everydayness' into something more unnervingly 'out of reach' (2006). Additionally, in his biography of Nicholas Ray, Patrick McGilligan (2011) constructs the 'normality' of Ray's upbringing through a direct alignment with the ordinariness of Ed/

Mason in this film, so at the very least, the sense of Mason as nothing but a destabilising 'foreign' figure should be questioned.[17] Additionally, Mason characterises *Bigger Than Life*'s failure in terms of individuality: *he* should have fought harder to insist on black and white, *his* casting was the problem, and so on. But they were also indicative of wider industry woes, as by 1956 many colour and widescreen films were performing poorly at the box office (Finler 2003: 120), and where the hierarchising of 'high' and 'low' art categories distinguished artistic and critical value according to genre, with *Bigger Than Life* being firmly placed into that of excessive melodrama (Mann 2008: 131).

Sheridan Morley describes the years between 1951 and 1956 as 'a golden period' where Mason finally had a run of financial success that brought him back from the wilderness. It is, of course, deeply ironic that this periodisation and measurement of success excludes

Bigger Than Life

Caught, *The Reckless Moment* and *Bigger Than Life*. The box office and poor reception of the latter film is usually positioned as the beginning of the end of Mason's Hollywood prospects, whereby Hitchcock's *North by Northwest* is the single respite before *Lolita* and the return to the UK. With the re-evaluation of Max Ophüls and Nicholas Ray as significant auteur directors, these works would become some of Mason's most critically acclaimed and important films. That through his star status and contract negotiations, Mason was such an instrumental figure in producing *Caught*, *The Reckless Moment* and *Bigger Than Life* adds value to the years previously considered career doldrums and the films that were initially categorised as 'lamentable failures' or 'heavy-handed issue movies' (Mason 1981: 277; Scheibel 2014: 183).

North by Northwest dominates discussions of Mason's post-*Bigger Than Life* Hollywood career, positioning it as indicative of his changing star status and economic value, comparing his $100,000 salary to the $1 million paid to Cary Grant (Morley 1989: 121). But Mason remained active beyond this, maintaining the mix of studio-based and independent filmmaking opportunities. He made one more film for the (now independent) Zanuck, *Island in the Sun* (1957), and in 1958 was reportedly offered £500,000 to make 'an Anglo-American film series based on *The Third Man* for television' (Evans and Thomas 1958). The same year, he worked with independent producer Andrew L. Stone on *Cry Terror!* and *The Decks Ran Red*. Both were moderate successes and Mason reflected positively on his reconnection with low-budget, artistically controlled independent productions, including in 1959 his first official British film for over ten years, *A Touch of Larceny*, produced by Ivan Foxwell. Meanwhile, Portland Pictures produced one final film, *Hero's Island*, a 'strange but interesting film' (review qtd. in Hirschhorn 1977: 155) that Mason remembers as having 'the same momentary success as *Caught*' (ibid.).

Europe and the UK 1962–84

Although Mason categorised the last third of his career as his British homecoming from Hollywood, the films made during these years were often co-productions between American, British and other European countries. He still characterised the move in terms of power, again expressing often contradictory views. In 1969, he presented Hollywood as a prize he failed to capitalise on, having 'to come back with my tail between my legs' (qtd. in Hirschhorn). Looking back on those years later, he says, 'my future lay in Europe' and positioned it as the new nexus of filmmaking (1981: 437). In 1962, one newspaper described Mason's star power as greater than it ever was: 'Now ... Mason is much more his own master, a gilt-edged international star who can work at will on either side of the Atlantic' (Wilson). Whilst hyperbolic in its celebration, there is evidence to support the claim that Mason maintained a control over his film appointments until his death despite, as biographical accounts often suggest, coming close to financial insolvency many times.

The range of American film offers he turned down in the latter stages of his career – years most commonly described as those where Mason took what he could get – illustrates this. In 1966, he rejected a role in a Curtis Harrington film, explaining that 'there could be no question of doing it for a reduced salary ... it would have to be a commitment for my $200,000 minimum guaranteed salary'.[18] In 1972, he turned down James Bridges' offer for *The Paper Chase* (a role then played by producer-turned-actor John Houseman, who won an Academy Award) (Houseman 1988: 459). The following year, he turned down Daniel Mann's bid to cast him in *Lost in the Stars* – part of the prestigious American Film Series which adapted major contemporary plays with notable performers and directors. Finance was the reason behind some of these decisions, as Mason apparently avoided films with US backing, preferring to work only on European co-productions or British films made with British money, such as *Spring and Port Wine* (Hall 1969).

Once more, Mason openly criticised the British film industry for being too reliant on foreign financial input and compromised by the monopolistic structure headed by Rank and EMI that tied distribution and exhibition together, strangling independent production (Edwards 1970). Contrary in his attitude once more, he argued for the American system: 'American anti-trust laws would never have allowed that absurdity to exist' (Webster 1982).

Despite his criticisms, between 1962 and 1984 Mason continued to have a remarkably varied career, making low- and big-budget films in mainstream and exploitation cinemas and television productions. He appeared in leading roles and supporting ones, playing a range of characters of every nationality from Australian (*Age of Consent*) to Mexican (*Bad Man's River*), and including George Smiley (*The Deadly Affair*), John Watson (*Murder by Decree*) and Magwitch (*Great Expectations* [1974]). He developed a significant collaborative relationship with director Sidney Lumet, making *The Deadly Affair*, *The Sea Gull*, *Child's Play* and *The Verdict*, worked with Michael Powell, Ismail Merchant and James Ivory, and the increasingly influential cult director Fernando Di Leo. He received two Best Supporting Actor nominations for *Georgy Girl* and *The Verdict*. Although conventionally seen as a footnote to wider discussions of Mason's stardom, his later career is far more noteworthy than this suggests.

But due to space, here I am deliberately concentrating on a set of films that have previously been used to indicate the star's waning status and control – his Italian exploitation films of 1970s. These films have often been grouped as minor examples of European exploitation cinema, and their low cultural status and Mason's supporting roles in them has led to their omission from histories of his career. (Although these elements, too, describe his Gainsborough films.) Between 1970 and 1976, Mason appeared in seven exploitation films: *Cold Sweat* (France/Italy), *Bad Man's River* (Italy), *Kill!* (Spain/Italy/West Germany/France), *The Left Hand of the Law/La polizia interviene: ordine di uccidere* (1975 Italy), *The Flower in His Mouth/*

Gente di rispetto (1975 Italy), *Kidnap Syndicate/La città sconvolta: caccia spietata ai rapitori* (1975 Italy) and *Fear in the City/Paura in città* (1976 Italy).[19] In all of them Mason played secondary roles, often figures of authority – government agents, corrupt businessmen, police commissioners, town elders and officials – but also eccentric and violent criminals.

Mason ignores all these films in his autobiography, Clive Hirschhorn's *The Films of James Mason* omits most of them and Sheridan Morley's history records only that Mason lowered his sights to make some Spanish low-budget films. This dismissal prevails in popular discourse, from Thomas Weisser (1992: 23) on spaghetti Westerns to IMDb amateur reviews, where the films or Mason's appearance in them are 'embarrassing', only explainable through financial necessity. The star was happy to confirm this in interviews, saying that he made so many 'bad films' because he owed so much money to Pamela after their divorce. But Mason's public statements should be taken with a pinch of salt (especially as he cited similar reasons for making *Caught* in 1949). He was paying Pamela £26,000 annually and avoiding heavy UK taxes by living in Switzerland. He made an average of three films a year (including six in 1975), was able to turn down prestigious projects in 1972 and 1973, and forwent a salary in favour of percentages for *The Sea Gull*. Between 1970 and 1975, he worked extensively outside exploitation cinema, including *Spring and Port Wine*, *Child's Play*, *The Marseille Contract* (1974), *The Mackintosh Man* (1973) (with Paul Newman and John Huston) and *Autobiography of a Princess* (1975). He also had extensive and 'lucrative' voiceover work during this period (Morley 1989: 102). Given the idiosyncratic frequency with which he rejected film offers based on unsuitable location and climate, filming near to Switzerland may have been a contributing factor to his choice of Italian roles. So, simply to characterise Mason's work in exploitation cinema through a lack of power (financial necessity and failure to manage his career successfully) is – at the very least – problematic.

It is more useful to place his work in the cinematic, economic and national contexts of the 1960s and 1970s Italian (co-)productions, especially their relationship to the Hollywood industry Mason apparently left behind. As part of the economic difficulties facing Hollywood from the late 1950s onwards, the industry looked to exploit growing European markets and saw involvement in co-productions as the way forward. Following the mass influx of American films into Europe after the end of World War II, the Italian, French and British governments attempted to limit the number of imported films allowed into circulation. The post-war British government opted for a levy on exhibition that was recirculated into British production, and France and Italy imposed quotas on foreign imports, blocking the earning potential of the already financially strained Hollywood producers (Nowell-Smith 1998: 4). To negotiate these measures – and mirroring Hollywood strategies of the 1920s and 1930s – producers in Italy and the UK opted for co-productions across Europe and with American companies, opening (or re-establishing) European branches of Hollywood studios. Italy was a focus for this, ushering in the era of 'Hollywood on the Tiber', and by 1967 Hollywood was spending $35 million to make American films in Rome. These included those categorised as 'Italian' but clandestinely funded by American companies, countering Italy's restrictive quotas, import taxation and credit benefits to 'national' productions (Eleftheriotis 2001: 103–06; Wagstaff 1998: 74–76). Whilst Mason was correct when he recognised his future lay in Europe, he was naive in his criticisms of where funding lay, especially when many of the films he made during this period (British and Italian) had American funding, including *Bad Man's River*, *Georgy Girl*, *Duffy* (1968) and *The Mackintosh Man*. The so-called 'economic necessity' of Mason's turn to European/Italian filmmaking was not his alone, but indicative of wider Hollywood strategies as the power struggle over profitable filmmaking practice was played out in Europe.

Between 1967 and 1975, the Italian film industry pursued an expansionist policy, and by the early 1970s Italy was producing more films than the US and had eclipsed Britain as the largest market in Western Europe. Many actors associated with Hollywood cinema were working in Italy during this period, having become extremely popular and ingrained in the Italian public consciousness via their work in the 1940s and 1950s – part of the immense recirculation of American culture in post-war Italy (Fisher 2011: 15). As such, Mason's Hollywood career would have had significant commercial value in this vast marketplace of the early 1970s. The films he made were primarily for the domestic Italian market, which had become increasingly reliant on the production of cycles of films called *filone* – most famously the spaghetti Western. The popularity of *filone* films meant guaranteed financing and exhibition from the distributors, giving them a large degree of control whereby they insisted on modes of seriality and familiarity (Wagstaff 1992: 249). Mason made one spaghetti Western, *Bad Man's River*, but was employed most in the *poliziotteschi filone*-crime/action dramas involving police authority and/or vigilante avengers: *Cold Sweat*, *Kill!*, *The Flower in His Mouth*, *The Left Hand of the Law*, *Kidnap Syndicate*, *Fear in the City*.

In histories of Italian national cinemas, growing attention paid to the importance of exploitation cinema has moved beyond the initial focus on the spaghetti Western and *giallo*.[20] Increasingly, the *poliziotteschi* is recognised as equally significant to Italian filmmaking of the 1970s, with its ideological reflection of a tumultuous national political scene. Related to and influenced by Hollywood vigilante dramas like *Dirty Harry* (1971), but no longer dismissed as Hollywood 'knock-offs', they inform studies of the interplay between exploitation and mainstream transnational cinemas.[21] Cross-national casting was a significant element of these films, drawing on the transnational market appeal of foreign stars and using them in the construction of meaning-making around corruption, authority and the inevitability of violence. Along with Mason, other notable actors appearing in *poliziotteschi*

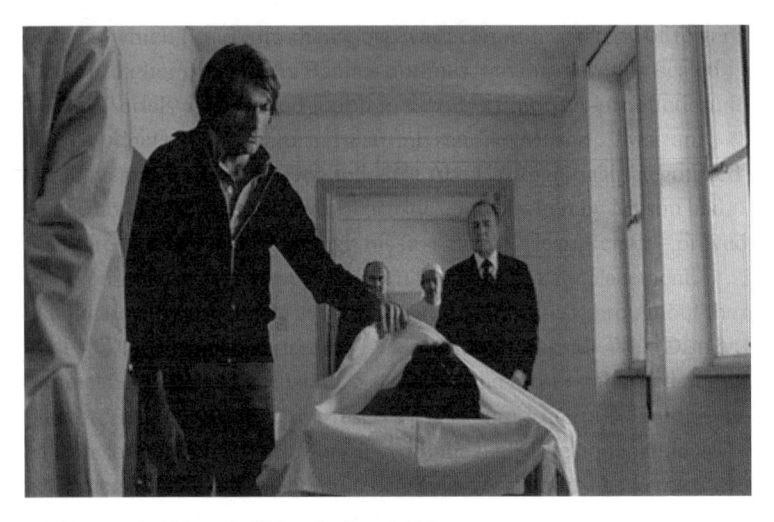

Luc Merenda and Mason in *Kidnap Syndicate* (1975)

were his co-star in *Cold Sweat* Charles Bronson, Oliver Reed, David Hemmings, Richard Conte, Henry Silva, Jack Palance and Joseph Cotten. Peter Bondanella discusses the use of iconic actors like Mason, Silva and Conte to communicate the thematic concerns and cultural positioning of these films. As well as discussing how Hollywood stars gave low-budget films more prestige, he explores Mason's film *Kidnap Syndicate*, citing how director Fernando Di Leo's casting serves the theme of the disparity between rich and poor (2009: 464). A business-like criminal syndicate kidnaps two boys – the father of one, Fabrizio (Luc Merenda), is poor; the other, hardened businessman Fillipini (Mason), is wealthy. When Fillipini attempts to negotiate a lower ransom, the syndicate kills Fabrizio's son and the film follows the violent revenge he metes out. Somewhat ironically – but perhaps illustrative of his status in Italy – Mason is cast as a symbol of absolute power in Italian society, as both Fabrizio and the police are powerless to act until Fillipini's say-so. Mason's performance is one of coldness and stillness (punctuated by mechanical gesture) that contrasts with

Merenda's emotional passion. Aged thirty-two, Merenda resembles the younger Mason (who was the same age in 1941–42), with his glowering dark brow, full lips and chiselled cheekbones, which hints at themes of how corruption develops and consumes older men. Mason is used to convey not only the privileged rich class that may be personified by Italian perceptions of the Hollywood elite, but also the stubborn, argumentative businessman engaging in redundant power play that characterised his own specific identity.

Mason made no further Italian films after 1976. The conventional narrative explains this via an upturn in his fortunes and critical/financial success that enabled him to regain control in the final years of his career. He is 'rescued' from the wilds of exploitation cinema to reclaim significant supporting roles in big-budget Hollywood films with major stars and directors: Sam Peckinpah's *Cross of Iron* (1977), Warren Beatty's *Heaven Can Wait* (1978), *The Boys from Brazil* (1978), with Gregory Peck and Laurence Olivier, *Murder by Decree* and the star-studded adaptation of Agatha Christie's *Evil under the Sun* (1982). Between the acclaimed role in *The Verdict* and 'fitting swansong' of *The Shooting Party* (1985), many final appraisals of Mason saw him as one of the most gifted screen actors of the twentieth century. But these years also coincide with the end of the popularity of the *poliziotteschi* cycle, a decline that reflected dramatic changes in the power structure of the Italian entertainment industry itself, sparked by legislation that deregulated the public television industry and enabled the development of a competitive private and uncensored provision. This caused a boom in the television industry at the expense of cinema revenues, a situation exacerbated by the sudden reduction in the number of film theatres (Bondanella 2009: 479). After 1976, there was little space for the type of Italian film Mason had been making: regardless of whether (apparently) Hollywood came calling again, he would have already been looking elsewhere for new opportunities. We should also remember that he was not exclusively working in low-budget cinema during this period.

This belies such articulations of Mason's career during the early 1970s through diminished power, and an understanding of his star power benefits from the developing critical studies of the history and form of Italian exploitation cinemas. Rather than dismissing Mason's European years as insignificant and indicative of his 'powerlessness', it is useful to explore him (and other stars) through this economic and industrial context. Just as the new histories of talent agents, independent stardom and transnational cinemas open up thought-provoking avenues by which we analyse traditional Hollywood and British stardom, so too do these histories of the political economy of (what have been considered) marginal cinemas.

4 PERFORMANCE

Throughout the previous chapters, Mason's performances of *self* have dominated, with his screen roles discussed more broadly in terms of type, star image and ideological meaning. In particular, as seen in Chapter 2, Mason's screen appearances have been considered through a sense of audience reception and symbolic interpretation – the appeal of doomed masculinity, and/or brutally attractive sadism, age and regional identity. This chapter builds on the notion of creative agency, not as in Chapter 3 through economic and industrial systems, but via the construction of performance through individual choice and learned skills, filmic technique, genre and collaborative practices, and the visibility of performative features across a body of work. Here, I shift focus onto the 'on screen' with an extended analysis of Mason's acting, considering gesture, voice and interaction, how these work with genre expectations and tone, the cinematic nature of the performances and their relation to filmic and directorial style, and the way these elements present particular affective positions to the viewer. This is not about defining Mason as a 'great' performer – as the retrospectives outlined in the introduction do – but about investigating the construction of film performance and the complexity of effect, technique, medium, individual physicality and intonation in creating this, and how these contribute to the star appeal of Mason. Throughout, I attempt to differentiate Mason's technique and creative labour away from the idea of Mason's *selfhood*, where the suggestion is that his performances reveal something about the 'reality' of the actor's life.

Pondering on his early success in *The Man in Grey*, Mason wryly surmised that his performance was due to his 'real' personality coming through on screen:

I wallowed in a black mood throughout [filming] and since my own imagination contributed nothing to the Lord Rohan who appeared on the screen, I have to conclude that only my permanent aggravation gave the character colour and made it some sort of memorable thing. (1981: 186)

But this is compromised by the similar performance and appeal of Mason as Nicholas in *The Seventh Veil*, a film he was immensely proud of and had much control over. Instead, Mason developed a particular way of performing these sadistic characters, and his reminiscence takes on a function that dismisses his acting in order to articulate an individual power struggle. Similarly, characterising his later performances in exploitation and low-budget cinema as reflecting another apparently 'real' state of mind – that Mason's acting was 'performed embarrassment' at appearing in unworthy films – is just as problematic. Consider the continuities that can be drawn between one of his most celebrated performances as Phillip Vandamm in *North by Northwest* and as Richard Straker in the adaptation of Stephen King's *Salem's Lot* (1979), directed by Tobe Hooper.[1] The scene in Hitchcock's film where Mason's Vandamm meets Cary Grant's Roger Thornhill for the first time (after having him abducted) and questions Thornhill over the identity of the fictitious spy George Kaplan has been widely analysed in terms of how the ironic distancing technique of Mason's theatricality conveys Vandamm's own play-acting as he stage-manages the scene, controlling lighting and spatial relationships.[2] Although a very different film, a similar performance occurs in *Salem's Lot*, where Mason's Straker – a mysterious figure (masquerading as an antiques dealer) assisting a vampire to bring death to small-town America – is suspected of involvement in the disappearance of a local boy and is questioned by the police constable Parkins Gillespie (Kenneth McMillan). Again, Mason's droll performance conveys the sense of the character's play-acting, making the same use of movement, stance and props as Vandamm in Hitchcock's film to communicate Straker's gleeful pleasure in fooling the officer. Mason moves through the space of his shop to sit behind an elaborate desk. He looks up at Gillespie, tilting his eyes towards him as he teases for information and casually bats away suggestions of his nefarious role, in doing so changing expectations of the power dynamic. Straker engages in wordplay to dominate further, and Mason uses precise, clipped enunciation to sharply dismiss Gillespie with a condescending 'ciao'. Mason even uses a prop in the same manner discussed by James Naremore in *North by Northwest* where Vandamm's nonchalantly twirled pair of glasses and cigarette are transformed into an expressive object (1988: 223); in *Salem's Lot*, the expressive object is an antique paper knife, similarly twirled.

To dismiss Mason's work in *Salem's Lot* as merely reflecting the actor's real-life 'contempt' for having to appear in the film – as one horror fan site does – belies the presence of skilful and repeated performative techniques that the star employed throughout his career.[3] This is typical of my approach here, examining some of Mason's lesser-known performances as well as more famous ones to think about the consistencies and deviations within his performative style. It expands on an observation made by David Hemmings (Mason's co-star in *Murder by Decree*) about the actor's technique: 'He never locked himself into any one characterization or role ... and therefore he remained totally professional but totally unexpected, and that was very exciting to work with' (qtd. in Morley 1989: 165). Therefore, this chapter also takes a different approach to structure than the previous ones; instead of following a broadly chronological structure,

Salem's Lot (1979)

I explore key concepts central to Mason's acting based on medium, genre, expression (vocal and physical) and affective position: Stage and Screen, Monologues and Silences, Tragedy and Comedy, and Intellectual Distance and Emotional Empathy. Each explores two contrasting elements to illustrate how Mason's performances negotiate each concept to offer an overview of his style, activity and employment.

Stage and screen

Typical of his generation, Mason's professional acting career began in the British theatre, where he toured in regional productions from 1931 to 1933. Following this apprenticeship, he worked at the Old Vic Theatre in London for two years under director Tyrone Guthrie, during which time he acted with – amongst others – John Gielgud,

Charles Laughton and Roger Livesey. At the end of 1934, he had a successful season at the Gate Theatre in Dublin, appearing in everything from Eugene O'Neill to Shakespeare, including Brutus in *Julius Caesar*. He played the same role in the 1953 film directed by Joseph Mankiewicz and was reunited with his former stage co-star, John Gielgud (who played Cassius).[4] Although his was never a career finely balanced between stage and screen, Mason had a keen interest in the theatre and maintained an infrequent presence there, including on the New York stage in 1947 in *Bathsheba*, and in 1979 with the first production of Brian Friel's *Faith Healer*. In 1954, he was invited by Guthrie to perform at the director's new project, the Stratford Shakespearean Festival in Ontario, Canada (which had begun the previous year with Alec Guinness), playing in *Measure for Measure* and *Oedipus Rex*. Both Mason and Guinness had been approached as part of Guthrie's business strategy of importing stars to raise awareness and the market value of the festival (Hunter 2001: 126).

Mason's stage appearances always garnered mixed reviews. Coming so soon after the run of major film successes, his Stratford work was particularly noted as being the wrong medium for the actor, as Mason's most famous tool – his voice – was not suited to the environment. His co-star Donald Campbell commented that although he underwent projection training, 'that very smoky voice which was so wonderful and distinctive on a film soundtrack was really terrible in a theatre, because it had no depth or variety' (qtd. in Morley 1989: 111). This mirrored Mason's own view that movie work had left his voice 'lacking in mobility and range' in comparison to those more used to the stage (1981: 311). Coupled with his perception that '*real* acting was practiced in a live theatre', the star had often expressed a very low opinion of his abilities as a performer (ibid.: 134). His work on *Julius Caesar* in 1953 seemed to crystallise this. Mason wanted the chance to repeat his earlier stage role and to work with Gielgud again, but felt immensely inferior to the critically acclaimed actor (who 'spoke with such richness and authority ... charged with such emotion') and fretted about his performance for years after (ibid.: 310–11).

Elements of these can be seen in the film: in comparison with Gielgud, Mason's posture is often quite stiff, with overly practised gestures and movements around the sets to underscore the words he speaks. There is also a lack of fluidity to his delivery, accompanied by wide-eyed unblinking that suggests effortful concentration and ill-ease with the speeches. During his oration to the masses the speech after Caesar's death, his voice is noticeably strained: 'Romans, countrymen, and lovers! hear me for my cause, and be silent, that you may hear …' However, this compromised flow and fluency works with the function of the scene and of Brutus' character in its representation of a conflicted figure losing control over the crowd, who rally instead behind the words of Mark Anthony (Marlon Brando) that follow: 'Friends, Romans, countrymen, lend me your ears.' Elsewhere, the soft closeness of a delivery practised through microphone recording effectively counterposes Brutus with Cassius. In Brutus' monologue that debates the necessity of Caesar's death, Mason uses an intonation that conveys thoughtful intimacy, aided by the unobtrusive accompanying string soundtrack. This contrasts with Cassius' preceding defiant words designed to motivate Brutus' involvement, which Gielgud delivers through quick and confident enunciation, complemented by a dynamic backwards tracking shot and sharp brass musical flourish.

Mason rated his performance poorly and as typical of his experiences with stage work. Elsewhere, it seemed to polarise critics, with some commenting that in trying too hard, he forgot to act and fell into verbal monotony, whilst others emphasised his intelligence and sincerity, noting that Mason created the character rather than having it imposed upon him (all qtd. in Hirschhorn 1977: 118). Away from the initial reviews, what becomes evident is how it was repositioned in terms of a *filmic* performance, indicative of the star's skills as a screen actor. Three-time co-star James Coburn described his appreciation of the performance in terms of its distance from traditional stage interpretations, saying 'all the others are playing Shakespeare and [Mason] is playing Brutus'.[5] He reflected more widely over Mason's

Mason with John Gielgud in *Julius Caesar* (1953)

technique and influence, highlighting the subtlety the actor brought to his work that was lost on set but rendered visible on screen in the scenes they played together:

you'd do your bit and then wait for his reaction, which didn't seem to come at all. Not at least until the next day, when you'd see the rushes and realize that he'd done it all, but so intimately that only the camera could pick it up. (Qtd. in Morley 1989: 146–47)

Neil Sinyard also identifies the power of Mason in close-up in Mankiewicz's film, where his otherwise subdued elements surpass Gielgud's overly emphasised theatrical reading in their shared shots (1986: 14). It is in the way Mason handled the performative space created by the camera, particularly in close-up, that reveals the effectiveness and range of his acting. Ironically, given the star's inferiority complex around Gielgud, the stage actor later noted how important the experience of working with Mason was in developing his own performance technique for the camera: 'James had much more to teach me on that film than I ever had to teach him. I used to observe his technique in the close ups, and saw how brilliantly he expressed his character's thoughts without making faces or grimacing' (qtd. in Morley 2002: 246). Although dismissive of himself, it is through the microphone, the photographic image and the cinematic frame that Mason's subtle technique of underplaying and his creative agency in the construction of a film's character, tone and texture becomes visible.

We can see this in Mason's performance as Norman Maine at the end of *A Star Is Born*. It was a performance widely acclaimed on the film's release, with Mason nominated for an Academy Award and reviews constantly highlighting his acting as part of the film's success. The *Motion Picture Herald* wrote that 'it is a role which tests the quality of an actor, for it has tones and shadings, highlights and shadows. Mason proves conclusively that he is one of Hollywood's finest performers' (Anon. 1954a), and *Film Bulletin* remarked that 'Mason is the surprise of the film ... he scores with such sincerity and realism one imagines he was born to the role' (Anon. 1954b). It is also the performance that has had the most in-depth scholarly attention, including Peter William Evans (2001), Amy Lawrence (2010) and Roberta Pearson (1999). Pearson offers a comparative analysis between Fredric March's portrayal and Mason's version in the 1937 and 1954 versions of the film. She reads Mason's performance through the intertextuality of his star persona, suggesting that interpretations of his acting rely on knowledge of Mason's image as the atypical, uncooperative foreign star, an image which sanctions his Maine as more intelligent and emotionally vulnerable than March's (71–72). Her conclusion that the former quality undermines the credibility of Mason/Maine's disintegration has been challenged by Lawrence, who, concentrating on the scene at the Oscars, argues that the depth of Mason's performance draws on humour, intelligence and contempt to communicate the aching desire, humiliation and failure of Maine as a figure powerless in the face of addiction (2010: 94). Whilst I want to avoid Lawrence's secondary reading of this as reflective of Mason's own Hollywood 'powerlessness', her analysis of Mason's practised construction of Maine is a perspective that I continue in my own consideration of his final close-ups in the film in order to illustrate the technical skills and creative agency that Gielgud so admired.

Following a relapse of his alcoholism and subsequent drunken disappearance, Norman Maine is handed over to the care of his beloved wife, Vicki Lester (Judy Garland). On waking from his stupor, he hears through an open window Vicki tell the studio head Oliver Niles (Charles Bickford) that she will give up her career to look after him, a sacrifice that drives Maine to despair. His realisation is filmed in a sustained close-up of Mason lying in bed that is overlaid and intercut with Garland and Bickford's conversation. The effectiveness comes from Mason's *performance-in-close-up*; it relies on the subtle expression, flow and pacing that the close-up reveals, and how it operates with the cross-cut shots of the conversation on the patio. Style and acting intertwine, with Mason's acting dictating the cinematic choices of director George Cukor, *mise en scène* allowing elements of the performance to come to the fore, and the editing contributing to the emotional intensity of the acting. As Cukor retells it, the creative agency in the sequence lay with Mason:

[the scene] was very moving ... but all the credit for that goes to James. He did it all himself. What I did was to let him do it and let it go on and on ... let the camera stay on him for an eternity. He became so involved that he could not stop ... and I let him do what he felt. (Qtd. in Emmett Long 2001: 23)

Although much of the emotive power comes from Mason's naturalism, other factors contribute significantly, including the cross-cutting and *mise en scène* in the contrasting set-up between the spaces occupied by Mason and Garland/Bickford. As entrapment and freedom form the subject of the conversation, they are visually represented too. Mason occupies an interior close space where the camera is tightly focused on a well-lit face, surrounded by a bed that is rendered a dark, abstracted and internalised space. Garland/Bickford are filmed together in a wide shot in the open space of the outdoor terrace, where the landscapes are emphasised as they stand in front of wide glass doors that reflect the ocean in front of them. Mason's scene is one of silence and virtual stillness, whereas Garland (and to a lesser degree Bickford) is in constant motion through the whole space, from her demonstrative gestures and raised, near-hysterical voice, to the constant fluttering of her scarf in the wind. The contrast helps to shape the flow of Mason's performance, as he uses an organic development of intensity, expression and physical opening-up as Maine moves through acclimatisation, realisation and then containment of his emotions. At one point, Mason makes a gesture that potentially disrupts this structure – he raises his hand to his forehead. This comes too early on in the scene to allow for that accumulation of emotional build-up, and Cukor cuts around it to counter its potential interruption. What this leaves is Mason's slow and subtle framing of expression and gesture as he moves from stillness and almost imperceptible facial changes to a more overt reaction that is violent both in its dynamism and repression. After Garland's line 'I love him', Maine awakens and orientates himself with stuttering blinking eyes and furrowed brow, moving from conforming to the early description of him as 'childlike' when sleeping to something more serious. A slight turn of the head upwards shows his acknowledgment of their conversation, but otherwise his body remains still and the shot is dominated only by minute eye movements as he contemplates Vicki's words, until the camera cuts back to the exterior space as Oliver comments that 'there's nothing left anymore'. Remaining still, Mason's eyes droop and soften on hearing this and his lips part with a tiny head movement as if to shake in disagreement to words he knows to be true. His eyes and mouth then open wider as Oliver continues and the camera cuts back to Vicki's reaction. On registering her determination to try to help him, Mason's intensity subtly increases. With his hand now to his forehead, pushing up his eyebrows and rocking his head gently on the pillow, his face becomes a space of open vulnerability as his attention shifts from his own weakness to Vicki's sacrifice. As Oliver says 'Goodbye Vicki Lester, hello Mrs Norman Maine', Mason looks up and mouths his surname in despairing realisation. This prompts a bigger physical reaction as he arches his head up the pillow, screws his eyes, moves his hand back and twists his fingers into his hair. These gestures begin to create an emotive tension that, as he buries his chin into his chest and then throws his head and arm backwards, seems about to be released. But it is all contained; instead of a scream, only a gasp escapes. A gulp in his throat, a series of strangled silent sobs, closed eyes with a tear trickling down the side of his face, trembling mouth show the depth of Maine's pain and realisation through Mason's reveal and then suppression of extremity and passion. The silenced sob continues as he turns to fall towards the pillow to conceal his face and the scene is enveloped in darkness.

Given the restrained subtlety of Mason's acting here, cataloguing specific gestures does somewhat belie the overall effect of the sequence, where the fluidity of the developing pace and scale, and the still, naturalistic qualities of Mason himself (especially in contrast to Garland's emotive acting), create a *sense* of character and emotion. This was recognised in Henry Hart's review: 'his facial movements and the gulp in his throat, when he decides to commit suicide, so completely actualize the ineffable – the death of the ego' (1954). When he assigned creative agency to the star, Cukor also believed that the sequence's power came from watching Mason *himself* disintegrate (Cukor described him as discrete, reserved and mysterious [qtd. in Emmett Long

A Star Is Born (1954)

(2001: 23)]). However, it is clear that the emotive effect comes from the filmic apparatus and scene construction itself, which works in collaboration with Mason's own screen performance technique, as much as from any performance of selfhood. Mason discussed his preferred acting style in terms of a combination of intelligent, intuitive and imaginative approaches that strived for identification and that were flexible, inasmuch as being tied to no one school of acting and aware of the objectives of the camera and filmmaker (1981: 411–12). This sequence acts as a useful combination of the interpretations of Cukor, Gielgud, Pearson and Lawrence on the typical elements of a Mason performance that go beyond a performance of star image, where his own creative agency, the relationship between this and the camera, and the intuitive and intelligent communication of character through performance style may be observed. Characters conveyed with a quiet devastation can be found throughout Mason's career as much as the overtly playful archness of films like *North by Northwest* and *Salem's Lot*.

Monologues and silences

The voice of James Mason plays a hugely significant role in his star appeal and screen performance style, with much consideration given to how he sounds in (or how the microphone records) accent, range, texture and intonation. Adrian Garvey (2015) has examined the complex and contradictory *sound* of Mason's voice, from the difficulty of defining it – collating critics' descriptions of it from 'steely velvet' to 'querulous and plangent' – to placing it as emblematic of his overall transgressive star persona and indicative of the trouble we have in locating Mason in terms of class, nation and power. Showing it to be warm *and* authoritative, fragile *and* strong, aristocratic *and* regional, romantic *and* earthy, whispered *and* forceful, excessive *and* subdued, Garvey's discussion illustrates how important studies of the voice are to understandings of star identity and performance. Throughout his career, Mason was afforded platforms that showcased his voice as a distinct performative tool, where many of his films provide space for monologues and speeches – Garvey looks at two significant examples from *The Pumpkin Eater* and *The Upturned Glass* – and it is the function of the *sound* and *silencing* of James Mason's voice (and the relationship between the two) that I explore here.

Such cinematic soundscapes are present from Mason's early films through to his last: from a recital in *Thunder Rock* to *The Shooting Party*, which opens with his words charting the end of an era, the rise of materialism and the threat of World War I. Mason orates to crowds – real and imaginary – in *The Upturned Glass*, *Odd Man Out*, *Madame Bovary*, *Bigger Than Life*, *Julius Caesar*, *A Star Is Born*, *Island in the Sun* and *The Marriage-Go-Round*. Often these lectures are used as a means of demonstrating how much his characters control the situation, with (as in *Julius Caesar*) the limitations of Mason's depth of tone and strained projection contributing to the film's meaning-making and communicating the failings of his characters – most famously in the scene at the Academy Awards in *A Star Is Born* where Maine interrupts Vicki's acceptance speech with his own desperate plea for work. When and where Mason is allowed to speak, and who interrupts that distinctive voice, becomes narratively significant: in *Island in the Sun*, his character's political ambitions are destroyed by a catastrophic speech that is continuously interrupted by his opponent (Harry Belafonte), who wins over the crowd with his smoother, deeper and more authoritative delivery.[6] When this internalised theme of power play is absent, Mason's lectures are noticeably weaker elements of his performance, such as the rather wooden commentary used in *The Marriage-Go-Round*, where the warring husband and wife team (Mason and Susan Haywood) explain their motivations to an unseen audience – what is far more interesting and engaging are the dialogue-heavy and physically farcical scenes of the domestic battle of the sexes that this narration bookends.

Elsewhere, Mason's monologues are indicative of the expectations and pleasures of the star's performances, where the distinct vocal aesthetics of his voice are emphasised through close filming and sound recording. As seen in his extensive radio and narration work, Mason's voice had commercial appeal beyond his films in the UK and US, including the eccentric travelogues *The London Nobody Knows* (1967) and *Home James*, and his biblical readings for Yorkshire Television's *Stars on Sunday* (1969–79). He also released two LPs of the *Poetry of Robert Browning* for the independent American company Caedmon in the mid-1950s. It was showcased even earlier in the surreal animated short *The Tell-Tale Heart* (1953) adapted from Edgar Allen Poe by United Productions of America (UPA) for Columbia Pictures. Here, the intimacy of the voiceover narrator suits the nuanced technique of Mason's intonation and juxtaposed soft/sharp qualities as he tells the story of a lodger compelled to murder his landlord and then driven mad with hallucinations of the victim's still-beating heart. Opening with forceful and firm diction that repeatedly stresses first consonants and certain words, '*T*rue I am *n*ervous, very *very* nervous. But *w*hy would you say that I am *m*ad? See how *p*recisely I tell the story to you. *Listen.*' This preciseness falters as the circumstances unfold: 'It s̲tarts with an o̲ld man, an o̲ld man in a ho̲use', which emphasises the lilting softness of the 's' and 'o' sounds. As the narrator falls further into paranoia and fear, Mason shifts between quick, harsh delivery to a more contemplative slow articulation to illustrate the unreliability of the commentary that drifts between sanity and madness. The absence of precise visual detail in the abstracted animation style reflects the disturbed state of mind and concentrates attention onto Mason's voice, whilst the close recording picks up every nuance in a carefully constructed and paced aural performance.

As widely celebrated as Mason's voice is to the appeal of his star persona and acting, also important is the absence of speech in his films and the function that these silences take on. In some examples where his characters are momentarily *silenced* by others, this is used to demonstrate a sense of destruction, decay and powerlessness. But in *Odd Man Out*, the silencing of Mason's voice, through the wound that seriously disables Johnny and his desire to remain hidden from the authorities, runs throughout the film. It is partly a means of distancing his appearance in Reed's film from his earlier roles and saturnine image that made use of his 'cultured, patrician [flat] enunciation' (Garvey 2015: 95). When he does speak, it is markedly different from expectations – a weak, whispered voice and gentle Irish accent. But Mason/Johnny's silence also serves a distinct thematic purpose, as it brings a sonic dimension to the film's expressionistic visual style where sound reflects his mental state, separating him from the noise and chaos of the city and suggesting that the doomed man occupies a different plane of existence as he makes his symbolic journey through the streets towards an inexorable death. Dai Vaughn suggests that Mason's meek delivery communicates from the start that something is fatally wrong with Johnny's leadership and conviction (1995: 17). Mason's silencing becomes indicative of the film's existential exploration of individual isolation, moral ambiguity and fatalist

Odd Man Out (1947)

philosophy, which, although challenged in Johnny's hallucinatory monologue in the painter Lukey's (Robert Newton) apartment that quotes Corinthians, ultimately prevails in the quietude and passivity of his cold and brutal death.

Although not necessarily an intentional reference, in terms of narrative arc and the silencing of Mason, there is an interesting parallel to *Odd Man Out* in the *poliziotteschi* film *Cold Sweat*. Mason plays Ross, the leader of a drug-smuggling gang that takes hostage the reformed criminal Joe (Charles Bronson), his wife and teenage daughter. As with Reed's film, Mason uses an accent (American – and as with his Irish accent, not an entirely convincing one), denying the viewer the emblematic sound of Mason. Unlike Reed's film, here his performance begins gregariously with an overplayed geniality that masks more violent intentions, but it too descends into silence and fatalistic contemplation. A disastrous attempted handover of the hostages results in Ross's trigger-happy accomplice shooting him in the stomach. In a visual set-up remarkably reminiscent of Johnny's framing in Lukey's flat, Ross spends the last third of the film weakly slumped silently in a chair in a decrepit shack, forced to face up to his slow, inevitable death. Recognising the futility and the inhumanity

Cold Sweat (1970)

of the situation he has himself created, he begins to protect Joe's wife and daughter from the perverted and murderous attentions of his increasingly desperate co-conspirator. In both *Cold Sweat* and *Odd Man Out*, Mason creates constricted, mostly silent performances of impotence that are juxtaposed with absurdist monologues (philosophically so in the latter film, more of a masqueraded identity in the former). And in both, there is little difference in the actor's performative technique which captures and conveys emotions in small facial expressions, heavy, clumsy posture and gesture, mournful eyes, disquieting accent and a refusal to articulate through sound to show the silencing of doomed men.

Peter William Evans' discussion of Mason (through his screen persona) as an existentialist figure positions the star as emblematic of philosophical debates about absurdity, sadism, free will and death bound up in the 1940s and World War II, where 'human beings are doomed to commit acts of horror and destruction … even as they attempt to construct a civilised world' (2001: 117). Although he characterises Mason's acts of destruction through the physical (beating, addiction etc.), which then inform the brutality of his persona, the interplay between silence and speech in his acting is also indicative of an existential state of being in his characters. As well as being silenced and acted upon, Mason's characters are also *wilfully silent*. They watch, evaluate and *are*, before they *act* to pass judgments on the past, the present and the future. *The Shooting Party* uses such interplay to position his character, Sir Randolph Nettleby, as the silent visionary aware of the instability of his world, observing it cross into the modern era through challenges to class distinctions, the threat of oncoming war and the construction of ideology. The juxtaposition adds credence to his character's words when he does speak and, tellingly, although the film begins with his monologue, it ends with an image of him frozen in contemplation as a younger voice reflects on his experience as a soldier in the war. Mason's is a restrained performance of quiet and mournful 'heroism' – an existential hero who *knows* the absurdity of life and the certainty of death – in line with Adrian Garvey's definition of his later performances as naturalistic and subdued (2015: 86).

But a more overt performance of the same themes of the inevitability of war and devastation that makes use of this juxtaposition can be found in *The Flower in His Mouth*. Contrasting with Garvey's analysis of the dislocated effect that Mason's stylised overplaying has in *The Pumpkin Eater* (2015: 92–93), here his sudden shift from silent observation to an excess of dialogue is designed to draw the spectator into the character's pain and anger – the existential act of destruction through verbal, not physical, violence. An American teacher, Elena (Jennifer O'Neil), arrives in a small Sicilian town and is embroiled into a murder plot that reveals the town's dark wartime past. Mason plays Bellocampo, the town's former patriarch and Elena's landlord. Quietly observant throughout the film, Bellocampo's initial benevolence gives way as Elena confronts him on his involvement in the murders and treatment of the poor. The restrained passivity of his previous scenes shifts into a monologue delivered in a heightened emotional register. He describes how he has taken revenge on the townspeople for rejoicing at the Axis's defeat in the war – the war his son died in – and how they desecrated the tomb of his brother in the violent chaos of their victory celebrations. Throatily croaked shouting conveys his upset state and anger, as he recalls yelling at an enemy aircraft overhead 'Shoot it down! Kill them!', before loudly and confusedly rambling about his son's death. This is shot in profile, with his eyes screwed up and his face in near darkness from the trees' shadows, mirroring the abstraction and focus on voice of *The Tell-Tale Heart*. The strained, tearful voice emphasises his elderliness and vulnerability here – the release of a long-bottled-up bitterness, as much lost in himself as recounting it to the audience of Elena. Mason's acting works neither to condemn nor support Bellocampo's actions – the register is too emotional to really distance us from the pain, but the dialogue shows the fallacy of his vengeance. The effect leaves us with an unsettlingly existential *nothingness*.

Also filmed in 1975, the Merchant Ivory production of *Autobiography of a Princess* uses the interplay between silence and speech to explore a more overt political perspective through objective and subjective constructions of history. A virtual two-hander performed by Mason and Madhur Jaffrey, the film is structured as a conversation between an Indian princess (in exile in London) and her father's former tutor, Cyril Sahib, as they watch home movies and reminisce on their apparent happy history in India. The two provide commentaries to the films and recount their own memories of life under the British Raj and her Maharaja father, before reflecting on the other's. The Princess's idealisation of her father and the system she grew up in is challenged by both Cyril's recollections and his silent scrutiny of her stories. From the beginning they are heavily contrasted, as she fills the room with intense – but ultimately empty – chatter, whilst he wordlessly moves around the space perusing her meticulous staging of it and the romanticised painting of her father hanging on the wall. Later, his gaze moves from the painting to the 'reality' of photographs and newspaper clippings detailing the scandal that led to the Maharaja's downfall. Although predominantly silent for the film's first half, Mason is given equal screen time, constantly looking over at the Princess as she speaks with a sombre expression, breaking only to laugh politely at her stories and ask the identity of figures on screen. That he has to gently correct her when she misremembers names is telling, both of her cluelessness and his sharp perception of the history; looking at the lavish palace decoration (begun, she says, in 1938) and asking after the designer, Cyril reminds her that he was Austrian not German. Although the Princess speaks, we are meant to question her perception of history. Nearly forty years later, she remains surprised that the designer left to 'go back to Germany' halfway through the task, at which Mason squarely turns his face to her with an incredulous expression, although he contains his comments with a sigh and gaze downwards at his lap.

When he does speak at length, it is first characterised by a vague, meandering commentary over the images as he remembers the culture shock of India. But in the final scenes, his memories fall into sharper focus as he articulates long-repressed recollections. As he begins this monologue, the camera tracks from a two-shot into a close framing of Mason alone. Off camera, she interrupts his story, but this time with a firm gesture that silences her, he decisively tells her to 'wait, please'. He describes a life lived in great 'luxury', able to do whatever he wanted, but 'most of the time he did nothing but lie on a soft bed rotting in heat and boredom'. Mason's delivery stresses two elements – reducing the sharpness of the 'uxury' of luxury into a low-toned, languid and overly indulgently soft sound ('*uschschoury*') and contrasting this with an emphasis on the higher-pitched, firm consonants of '*n*othing', '*r*otten' and '*h*eat'. As it follows the soft sounds, the emphatic enunciation here dramatises suppressed emotions amidst an objectively privileged existence. This interplay enables a shift in the power relations; as his attention turns back to the projection, he now commentates authoritatively on the images. Later, the conversation turns to the end of her father's rule, where infidelity and blackmail led to his deposition. As the Princess talks of his innocence and her anger rises, Cyril blusters next to her and she challenges him over his taciturnity: 'Well, why don't you speak?' He walks away and holds his silence. She continues, 'When it is time for you to speak, you are silent. Now and at that time … Just another stab in the back – you can't deny it.' After the accusation, he finally demurs with a defiant 'I *can* deny it,' and a more gentle, 'If I had, who would have listened.' As a further monologue recounts his troubled relationship with the Prince, the thematic function of silence and speech moves from being concerned with the overtly political to reflecting on how the personal and subjective affect what unfolds into major historical events, intertwining the two. However, whilst it uses Mason's and Jaffrey's naturalistic and emotionally driven performances to communicate the significance of cultural memory, the film's central concern remains more political than personal in its dramatisation of post-colonial identity.

Tragedy and comedy

Traditionally, Mason is associated more with genres of drama and tragedy than comedy, from the dark 'doomed masculinity' of *Odd Man Out*, *A Star Is Born*, *Bigger Than Life* to the romanticised brutality of the Gainsborough melodramas and *The Seventh Veil*. These films employ performances that simmer with repressed emotional states of lust, power, fear and despair, conveyed by Mason's repeated performative traits of speech, expression and movement. He shifts from gritted and strained delivery to a more forceful and authoritative speech pattern that emphasises downbeats to show dominance in closed-down conversations. There is also contemplative stillness of expression as the camera lingers on his impassive face. This is countered not only by changes in voice, but also in revealing physicality, such as the way Mason often places a hand tightly around the necks of others during conversation in a gesture that exposes an underlying violent or needful tendency, contained in otherwise conventional embraces. Such acting aligns with genre expectations in their communication of unspoken desires and subtextual meaning, but elsewhere tragedy and comedy collide, and it is Mason's skilful negotiation of the two genres and registers that I now explore.

In generic comedies, the techniques and associations described above are used to add gravitas and urgency to anchor otherwise humorous narratives. In the heist caper *11 Harrowhouse* (1974), Mason plays Watts, a lowly employee of a diamond syndicate (run by John Gielgud) central to the ambitious robbery plans of Howard Chesser (George Grodin). The film's tone is brash and farcical, from Grodin's spoof-noir commentary and Trevor Howard's hammy performance as a millionaire antagonist, to the excessively destructive car chase that concludes the film. By contrast, scenes in which Mason/Watts appears are typified by a quietly powerful dignity and resolve. Watts' involvement is motivated by a diagnosis of terminal cancer and a desire that his family are provided for afterwards There is no sense of irony or archness to Mason's underplayed performance, which rests on depicting the banality of the tragic circumstances, as seen when Chesser tells Watts of the plan. Set during Watts' lunchbreak, the two sit in a park shelter framed in a medium shot where they are visually bisected by a pillar. Grodin looks across at Mason, but Mason looks ahead blankly. Watts' thought process is almost entirely communicated through the way Mason eats his lunch, chewing slowly and deliberately on half a sandwich. The pace of the chewing changes depending on the subject of conversation: stopping when Watts' 'time left' is mentioned, quicker when the plan is revealed and slower when Chesser emphasises his importance. His dialogue is delivered in a cracked whisper that creates a politely disinterested demeanour of stage-managed professionalism: 'But how can I help you, sir?' Only a single deliberate look across, look ahead and slow chew belies this. When Grodin places an advance payment of £250,000 on his knee, a worried but excited expression crosses his face and – at odds with the frenetic energy and insouciant attitude of the other characters – he softly blurts out, 'Oh, this is too much … even for that.' Although embarrassed by the sum, he looks at Grodin and – continuing the themes of banality and sandwich-as-subtext – deliberately covers it with his remaining cling film-wrapped half sandwich to acknowledge his acceptance.

The interplay between genre and performance/text and subtext is also present in Mason's performance as Trigorin in Sidney Lumet's 1968 adaptation of Chekov's *The Seagull*.[7] Although the play is ostensibly full of tragic events and characters, Chekov's insistent definition of his work as a comedy through its subtextual and thematic content requires intelligent and subtle unpicking of role and representation. During the course of the film, Trigorin, a successful and self-obsessed writer, leaves his mistress Arkadina (Simone Signoret) for a young, innocent woman Nina (Vanessa Redgrave), who worships him and his celebrity. The tragedy of their ensuing relationship – their child dies, her acting career fails, he eventually tires of her and returns to Arkadina – is undercut by never witnessing these events, only hearing about them through a wry, bitter and quick commentary by Konstantin (David Warner), Arkadina's son, Nina's former lover and failed writer. Here, the warmth and engagement of Mason's naturalism is used to create the subtle undertones that help position Chekov's work as comedy, not in the way it is used in individual scenes but when viewed across the whole text. On first meeting Nina, Mason's low-key acting conveys Trigorin's nervousness, avoiding eye contact, absentmindedly tapping his stick down as a diversionary tactic and then watching her from afar. In contrast, in the next scene, he confidently lectures her about the emptiness of fame, the meaninglessness of happiness, his compulsion to write and the attitudes of his critics, concluding that 'The public reads it and says: "Yes, it is clever and pretty, but not nearly as good as Tolstoy."' It is filmed in one take and throughout it, Mason circles

Redgrave and the space they occupy. He combines the restless frustration of the movement with a droll, self-assured delivery and a mocking tone as he loudly acts out voices and half smiles at Nina with an affectionate twinkle in his eye. The performance's qualities mirror Arkadina's later description of the character as she seduces Trigorin once more: 'You are so fresh, so simple, so deeply humorous. You can bring out every feature of a man or of a landscape in a single line, and your characters live and breathe.' He responds, 'I have no will of my own.' Mason's embodiment of this existential position, which was so crucial to the tragedy of *Odd Man Out*, is here used more comically as he lies on their bed, Arkadina on top of him mussing his hair up. The naturalistic genuineness of this moment is repeated again with Nina, when – about to leave with Arkadina – Trigorin spies her and gives her an address in Moscow where they can meet. The moment is one of intense romantic vulnerability, with barely contained desire in his hurried delivery and close embrace as he gently caresses Nina's face, describing her beauty and angelic purity.

Much of Chekov's comedy comes from the self-inflicted misery of his characters and their inherent ridiculousness, and Mason's performance communicates this about Trigorin. He is led by the women in his life and each time is genuinely moved by them – and their adoration of him – but mirroring his circular walk, he repeats the actions and learns little. He counters each moment of natural expression by adding observations about the scenes – both as commentary on and abstraction of the spontaneous emotional outbursts and romantic desires. By the end of the film, reconciled with Arkadina, Mason abandons the lightness of his earlier delivery, instead returning to his more typical intonation of dominant superiority with heavily stressed initial consonants – saying to Konstantin, '*Y*our *m*other tells me you're prepared to let *b*ygones be *b*ygones, and are not angry anymore.' Here, and in his following critique of Konstantin's writing, there is a sense of Trigorin-as-performer: he has unwittingly become one of the critical voices he role-played for

Nina in his monologue. There is nothing inherently comic in Mason's performance in the film, but the juxtaposition between shyness and confidence, expressive warmth – given to different women – and the sullen role play at the end works in harmony with the wider thematic concerns of Chekov's exploration of self-deluding comically tragic characters, where tonal register and genre are subtly at odds with each other.

In other films, Mason creates broad comedy through precisely worked-out physicality and deft comic timing. Comic physicality is not something commonly associated with Mason; more emphasis is placed upon the richness of his voice, his beauty and use of subtle expressions, but there are films that locate comic effect in Mason's body. This is most evident in the actor's later appearances in films with older men/younger women narratives: *The Marriage-Go-Round*, *Age of Consent*, *Georgy Girl* and *Lolita*. The first two rely on a lightness in Mason's acting to ground the pursuit of his characters by amorous young ladies where he can both reject and enjoy their attentions – casually farcical in *The Marriage-Go-Round* and more naturalistic in *Age of Consent*. The comedy of *Georgy Girl* comes from the contrast between his awkward yearning for Georgy and her spontaneous energy and reluctance to reciprocate, but the black comedy of *Lolita* offers the most complex use of Mason's comic timing and physicality. Like *The Sea Gull*, Kubrick's adaptation of Vladimir Nabokov's novel about the paedophilic desire of Humbert Humbert (Mason) for the eponymous teen nymphet is not a straightforward comedy; unlike Chekov's work, the excess of the comic elements work against the darkness of the subject matter and challenge the ostensible 'tragedy' of Humbert's loss of Lolita. Following the novel's first-person perspective (never presenting Humbert as simply repellent), how Mason shifts between these registers over the course of the film adds to Kubrick's overall effect that denies the viewer clear identification figures in its creation, and undermining, of a connection with the protagonist.

Shelley Winters noted how Mason arrived on set 'not as himself at all, but already as Humbert' (qtd. in Morley 1989: 132), and the star himself recorded the extensive preparation that afforded a long lead-in rehearsal time and improvisational approach (1981: 431). Although *Lolita* is framed by Humbert's voiceover, much of the comedy is created through the performance of character interactions and the management of physical space, body and dialogue, with Mason at its subversive centre. In comparison with the overplaying of Shelley Winters as Lolita's crass suburbanite mother and Peter Sellers as the mysterious Clare Quilty, who pursues Humbert and Lolita, Mason's underplaying constructs Humbert as a straight man, but one often at the nexus of the comic action. The opening sequence where Humbert shoots Quilty in his mansion is dominated by Sellers' excessive improvised speech, movement and use of props, including the ping pong game he insists Humbert joins him in. What is funny is Humbert's confused response: standing stiffly at the table, paddle in hand as if engaging in the surrealness of Quilty's world, he then ignores the balls. The inaction compared with Quilty's relentless action is the disruptive moment and it aligns the viewer with Humbert; we too are confused and disorientated by Sellers/Quilty's freneticism. When repeated at the end of the film, the scene's meaning changes. Mason's underplaying and unwavering gaze at Quilty becomes indicative of Humbert's passivity and ridiculousness as revealed over the course of the film. By the end, Humbert's tragic desire and revenge becomes the blackness of the comedy.

But we first laugh *with* Humbert, sharing in his frustrations as he moves through the satirical examination of American suburban attitudes in his relationship with Charlotte and her social circle, as illustrated in the scene of the town's Summer Dance. Trying to watch Lolita in peaceful isolation, Humbert is cornered on the balcony overlooking the dance floor by Charlotte and her friends Jean and John. As the conversation progresses, the frame becomes increasingly claustrophobic as the three of them stand over him, and he can only look on helplessly, trapped by the ambition of his landlady to get him alone. Mason has few lines during this scene, communicating the physical and narrative domination of Humbert through expression, position and prop. His posture slumps and he awkwardly holds a drink and plate of cake up at shoulder height almost in surrender, continuing to gaze firmly at Jean as she unveils her plan to create a romantic space for the two as, behind him, Charlotte debates it. As she excitedly agrees, he gazes up at her in subtle horror before looking down in irritation. As Jean begins to say goodnight, he blinks repeatedly and tries to stutteringly interject with an offer of supervision. He then moves to stand up in a gesture of power, but all three immediately place a hand on his head and each shoulder, pushing him down as he grimaces in defeat. He turns in his seat trying to persuade Charlotte to agree with him, but the hands remain on him and, as his annoyance rises, he tries to quickly shrug them off, caught up in his irritation at their insistent matchmaking. There is an

Lolita (1962)

alignment between Humbert's comic discomfort in the face of others' easy domination and our own understanding and acceptance of this.

But Humbert is not a figure of identification, and Mason's acting conveys how the attitude towards the character changes across the second act of the film – where Lolita is sent to camp, he marries Charlotte, she discovers his secret, is run over and dies. Here, Mason's underplayed style begins to recede in favour of a more overt approach, opening up the character's actions to questioning from the viewer and shifting the blackness of the comedy from suburban satire more fully onto Humbert himself. His reading out loud of Charlotte's love letter to him becomes more performative, arch and mocking in tone, overly expressive (pressing his tongue against his teeth) and finally overtaken by hysterical laughter. We are still laughing with him, but increasingly the laughter is more uncomfortable and disquieting.

In the end, we laugh *at* Humbert – a man now figured through a pathetic, lost and dishevelled state. Throughout the third act, the comedy comes from his violent mismanagement of events that he should now control. Ilsa J. Bick discusses the use of comedy here as more aggressive, with Humbert as the 'butt of the film's joke' in the wake of his increasingly sado-masochistic and subjugated actions, and she suggests that through their excesses such sequences lose their humour. Slapstick comes to typify the later 'comic' moments, but they function to disguise darker elements, most noticeably the pantomime with the hotel porter to set up the cot without disturbing Lolita's sleep which masks 'the very earnest and serious attempts of Humbert to get into bed with Lolita' (1994: 14). The physical comedy continues in the sequence where Humbert loses Lolita to Quilty during her stay in hospital. Separated from her, ill and alone in a motel room, he is woken by a telephone call from an unidentified Quilty. Mason's performance is incredibly broad: he clumsily knocks over crockery and the telephone itself, and, on answering, contorts himself into the bed's blankets, pulling them up over his head.

Lolita

What was a comical use of props in the Summer Dance scene now becomes illustrative of Humbert's inappropriate behaviours and responses; no longer the suave intellectual trapped by overbearing people but a man rendered obviously infantile and pathetic by his singular inability to handle a duvet. Afterwards, he rushes to the hospital and, on learning that Lolita has been discharged into the care of her 'uncle', causes a commotion that is violently suppressed by doctors and security. The ineffectualness of his fight is humorous, emphasised by the long framing of the scuffle down the hospital corridor, the close-up on his unkempt face as he is held down in a strange position, and the ridiculously smooth politeness with which Mason conveys Humbert's sudden agreeability. It is the trajectory from straight man to the joke that prevents his emotional breakdown in his final meeting with Lolita from becoming an emotionally affective tragedy of a protagonist we have followed closely through the film; instead, the increasing excesses of Mason's performance render Humbert absurd.

Intellectual distance and emotional empathy

Between his performances in *A Star Is Born* and *Lolita*, Mason conveys two positions – the former designed ultimately to move the audience emotionally and the latter to hold them at a distance. The duality is also contained in his vocal apparatus – the 'steely velvet' voice that is both taciturn and inviting, and the effect the absence and presence of his voice has on his roles. Both Peter William Evans and Amy Lawrence explore how the combination of this acting style and star image often worked as a sardonic and sceptical commentary on the roles he was playing, with Evans seeing this as part of the star's exciting yet sadistic appeal (2001: 110), whilst Lawrence places it as integral to the critically investigative stance his characters (and he) took towards American institutions amidst personal emotional suffering (2010: 86). Both discuss this explicitly in relation to Mason's appearances in melodrama during the 1940s and 1950s, particularly the cold brutality of the much-loathed Gainsborough films and the detached reflection upon his Hollywood career via the emotionally vulnerable characters of the aestheticised *A Star Is Born* and *Bigger Than Life*. As discussed, in *Lolita* and *North by Northwest* too these opposing elements are used to separate role from performer and audience. The technique is also a vital component of Mason's two films with Max Ophüls – a director associated with creating detached perspectives via filmic techniques of camera movement and depth of field photography to critique American society and ideology – *Caught* and *The Reckless Moment*. Laura Crossley (2014) notes how Mason's characters are the figures through which the critique is most explicitly voiced, emphasising how his star image as the 'odd man out' apart from conventional society informs this.[8]

In both films, Mason is used to create the intellectual distance through which Ophüls views the world, notably in the lack of close-ups, preferring to place him in set-ups where the camera moves dynamically through spaces or holds the characters at length. Examples of this visual organisation in *Caught* are discussed in detail by Mason, who describes his willingness to forgo 'star-like' close-ups or shot-reverse-shots of address and reaction – which Ophüls called 'rabbit shots' (1981: 272) – allowing Ophüls to construct complex set-ups using tracking shots and depth of field photography to create a sense of visual detachment, especially in scenes that involve conversation. Mason is often positioned in the background of scenes shot with depth of field, isolating him (and the character's reactions) from the viewer. This aligns him with the camera (and the distanced perspective contained therein) as it follows his movement through the doctor's surgery set, passing through walls and rooms, and later tracks him and Leonora dancing through space in a nightclub as their relationship deepens and he proposes marriage. Mason's performance mirrors this visual detachment through his use of an emphatic, almost instructive, tone in Quinada's interactions with Leonora that adds an aloofness and judgment to his conversation in spite of his character's ultimate role of the romantic saviour. Even his proposal to her in the dance hall takes on a rehearsed ritualised tone (despite the relaxed physicality of their laughing and dancing and the elaborately fluid tracking shot through the space), when, following her initial hesitance, he says, 'I'll propose again tomorrow.' Whilst this is scripted, the sense of ritual in the preceding lines comes from Mason's performative choices (which Ophüls then kept in the take): as they dance through the space, losing and reappearing in front of the camera, Mason repeats his lines about 'going out again on Saturday ... and spend Sunday together', which undermines the proposal as a natural and spontaneous emotional reaction. Ophüls has been characterised as an 'ironic director because of the obvious patterns of camera movements, repetitions of dialogue and other details ... invite us to distance ourselves from some events, pass judgements on particular characters, or reflect on an abstract "meaning" through doubling and directorial surrogates' (White 1995: 12), and here, the coldness and ironic commentary that Mason's acting and persona bring to the film are used to enhance these features of the director's work.

But this externalised detachment is not inherent in Mason's acting, even if it is a significant element of his star image. In Sidney Lumet's spy thriller *The Deadly Affair*, the performative, image-based intertextual commentary is downplayed in favour of a technique that juxtaposes distance and emotion to create character development and identity. Lumet saw the potential coldness of Mason's acting as a powerful tool in a film's structure and meaning-making. In an interview about working with Rod Steiger (whom he directed in *The Pawnbroker* in 1964), and reflecting on what Mason could have brought instead, Lumet commented that the difference between the two actors was that Steiger was '*in*capable of feeling *nothing*', whereas '[Mason could have been] even more detached ... Mason could have literally gone so dead inside that when the eruption came it would have been terrifying' (qtd. in Cunningham 2001: 294n).[9] Whilst this quality is present in Mason's other collaborations with Lumet, the star's work on *The Deadly Affair* draws on a more complex interplay between emotional revelation and detachment than this quote – and Cunningham's own analysis of the performance as a 'balance of coldness and desire' – acknowledges (ibid.: 37–41). *The Deadly Affair* is an adaptation of John Le Carré's novel *A Call for the Dead*, the first to feature George Smiley. (Following *The Spy Who Came in from the Cold* [1965]), Paramount Pictures retained the rights to Smiley's name, so he is renamed Charles Dobbs.) Mason's acting here matches closely Sue Harper and Justin Smith's analysis of the star's later performance in *Spring and Port Wine* in its reliance on the nuance of expression and movement through space. As they suggest, it is not a singular mode of 'character' acting but one of great flexibility that develops out of long personal experience of empathy (2012: 185). Mason's focus on the empathetic is still a performative position taken by the actor towards character and diegetic world – just as the cold detachment is – and this is foregrounded in the way he moves between the two presentational stances during the film in his construction of Dobbs.

The film begins with Dobbs interviewing Fennan, a member of the Foreign Office accused of being a Communist spy. When Fennan apparently commits suicide, Dobbs resigns from the secret service to conduct his own investigation. This is paralleled with scenes of Dobbs' troubled marriage and his wife Ann's many affairs, including one with their mutual friend Dieter Frey (Maximilian Schell), whom Dobbs recruited into the secret service during the war. Dobbs' investigation reveals that Fennan was murdered by Frey and Fennan's widow, Elsa, (Simone Signoret) who are both East German agents, and that Frey used the affair with Ann to gain intelligence on Dobbs. Lumet's film version added the subplot of the affair between Dieter and Ann, changing the name of the text to reflect this, and including a number of scenes between Dobbs and Ann and/or Dieter, creating the dual narratives of Dobbs being betrayed by those closest to him.

These scenes advance the book's thematic subtext of the interrelationship between personal and professional spheres, and are anchored around Mason's portrayal of the conflicted protagonist's inability to keep the two separate, and how Lumet's direction creates visual environments in which the conflict unfolds. Counter to Lumet's earlier description of Mason's acting, here the star does not initially employ a detached performance of simmering tension that builds across the film into an explosive eruption of emotion, nor does he simply balance one register against another (a coldness in his professionalism; an expressiveness in his personal life). This performative choice illustrates the fallacy of Dobbs' own desperate desire to keep his two worlds apart. The character tries hard to construct a detached demeanour: calm, thoughtful and professional in the face of the investigation and around Ann's infidelity, but the sense of emotional vulnerability permeates both.

Although he strives to occupy extremes, Dobbs is actually situated in a series of middle grounds (emotionally, physically, professionally and even in class terms). This is aided by Mason's swift movements between registers that – unusually – do not create tension between the two: never totally cold only to explode at the end; never destroyed by a vulnerability that completely closes him off at the narrative's conclusion. This performance is interwoven into Lumet's handling of formal space to reflect the uneasy liminality of the Cold War world. Perhaps the two most liminal spaces are Elsa's house and the hospital ward that Dobbs is confined to after being beaten during the investigation. In his first interview with Elsa, the official questioning is momentarily derailed by a tangential discussion about marriage where Elsa becomes the interrogator, asking Dobbs whether he possesses his wife. Mason's delivery of the response – 'I don't possess her; I love her' – uses a deep downward force on the 'pos' of 'possess' to imply the distance between his and the widow's emotional engagement with marriage, but the softness of 'ess' with an elongated 's' sound also tinges the word with regret. He then emphasises 'love' with a lilting intonation of acceptance and anxiety that this might be a weakness.

The interplay between strength and weakness continues in the hospital. Initially a site of physical vulnerability (Dobbs is laid up in bed with a broken arm), it becomes a place of professional forward momentum in the investigation that belies the visual construction of Dobbs' helplessness, recumbent as Mendel and Appleby – his co-investigators – dominate the space standing over him. Later, it becomes an emotionally resonant space when Ann visits her husband and tells him she's leaving him for Dieter. He first deflects Ann's concern that his investigation led to his injuries with a resigned 'No, I was getting drunk', underscoring a defeatism in his work and relationship. As she breaks the news to him, the camera tracks in to a close-up of Mason's reaction. The set-up closely resembles the staging of his breakdown scene in *A Star Is Born*. Here, Mason's depiction of the total disintegration of the character occurs more quickly and with even less expression than the earlier film, yet Dobbs' pain is palpable. His eyes glaze with moisture and only the slightest movement of eyebrows and mouth connote any changes in thought as he listens.

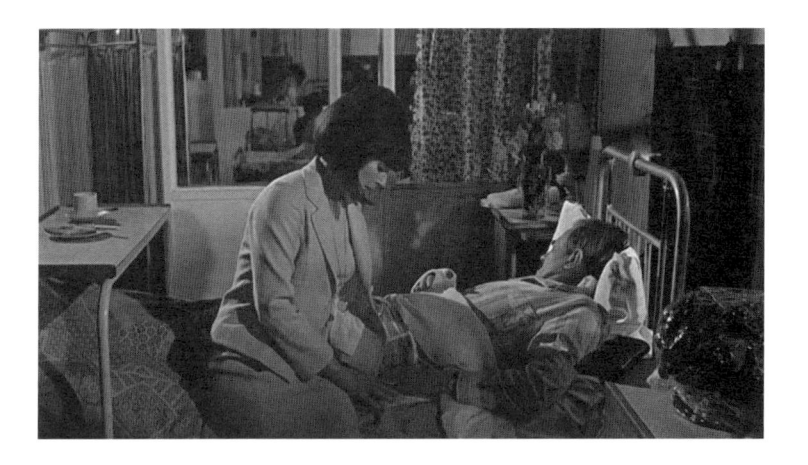

The Deadly Affair (1966)

As Ann offers him a kiss goodbye, he turns away and buries his head in the pillow, although – unlike *A Star Is Born* – due to the sharply overstated movement and wide framing, it appears as a response of deliberate stubbornness to distance himself from her. After she leaves the ward, he composes himself and delivers another ritualised line of detached concern: 'Don't fly if there's a fog.' Mason's response shifts between the subtle expression conveying Dobbs' genuine upset and two modes of role play (overbearing concern and petulant overemphasis) that act as his own mechanisms of intellectual distance.

Where the personal and professional intersect most is in the figure of Dieter. As played and filmed, the connection between Dieter and Dobbs is never wholly marked by distinct professional boundaries despite this being the origins of their relationship, as the scene that reveals Dieter as the enemy spy illustrates. This takes place in the theatrical space of the Royal Shakespeare Company; Dobbs is seated up in the balcony watching Elsa meet her contact (Dieter) in the stalls below. Spatially they are separated, seemingly occupying professional, politically divergent extremes – good and evil; East and West. This is also reflected in their countenance: Dieter is detached from everything – he kills Elsa without emotion and he does not see Dobbs – whilst Dobbs is a close observer of Dieter, never shifting his gaze. But the political and the emotional intertwine in Dobbs' reaction to the traitor's arrival in the theatre. It causes in him a spontaneous physical and emotional reflex: in shock, he starts to vomit and has to race to the bathroom (where he more or less composes himself). It is such an unexpectedly intense reaction, partly because Mason is rarely this violently visceral in his representations, but it is immensely effective in communicating Dobbs' vulnerability at the betrayal. It is disquieting in its emotional effect on the viewer, but the disturbance does not distance us from the character. Unlike Lumet's earlier words, it is not a *terrifying* effect whose power comes from occurring nowhere else in Mason's acting, but one that is powerfully affective because it has already been set up in this performance as the relationship between Dobbs and Dieter and Ann, and his professional boundaries have been examined by actor and filmmaker. Whilst Mason – in terms of acting and star image – is associated with conflict, duality and juxtaposition, *The Deadly Affair* makes use of these features to construct a performance around the intersection of different layers to create emotional resonance rather than a coldly distant portrayal created through the shocking collision of contrasting elements.

One of Mason's co-stars in *Odd Man Out*, Dan O'Herlihy (Nolan), later reflected on the star's performance in Reed's film, saying, 'What made James so good is that inside himself he was already on the run' (qtd. in Gilbey 2003). The assumption is clear – the tension embodied by James Mason came from within the star himself; to understand the performance, we must first understand the man – his anxieties, his lack of belonging, his sense of powerlessness. Throughout this chapter I have shown another layer to this: that contrasting positions were part of how Mason (and his collaborators) deliberately staged his performances throughout his career, often resulting in very different effects across a large body of work. At times this technique is most visible in his later roles beyond 1960, drawing more fully on comedy, silence and empathy in addition to the existential, cold, violent rebelliousness suggested by his dominant star persona. Mason's acting is never wholly naturalistic; there is always a sense of presentation or representation to be found in his characterisations. Whilst it can be as stylised as it is nuanced, it is also rarely excessive in tone, movement or delivery. These techniques and the interplay between them create an effect that is not always overtly one of *tension* a word I used to describe Mason in the introduction to this book but perhaps might be better described as one of *dissonance*, best used in films that resist aligning each element in harmony or resolution. As much as Mason may have been the Odd Man Out, an identity loaded with cultural meaning, he was also just 'odd'. Rather than always holding contrasting elements in sharp tension with each other, through image, power and performance, he also occupied spaces and identities that were somewhere in the middle: not ordinary/extraordinary but rather (like his appearance in *The Making of the Shining*) incongruous and unexpected.

NOTES

1 Introduction

1 Graeme Turner writes about the 'circular and reciprocal relationship between the academy and media', although positions this as indicative of a contemporary perspective and interest in modern celebrity culture. He discusses how the press use scholars' work to 'legitimate' their stories, whilst scholars mine them for empirical or textual detail (2010: 15).

2 Persona

1 Mason had a long association with the Brontës. He played Heathcliff on stage in 1935 and was approached in 1938 by Hollywood for the role of Hindley (Wyler papers, Margaret Herrick Library, Beverly Hills, California). In 1945, Mason had planned to play Bramwell in a film about the family (Mason 1981: 201), and in 1955 was in talks with Darryl Zanuck to play Mr Rochester in *Jane Eyre* (ibid.: 374–75).
2 Although not produced by Gainsborough, Mason had first played a similar type of character in *The Night Has Eyes* (1942).

3   The exception is the ghost story *A Place of One's Own* (1945).
4   Cf. Pam Cook (1996) and Marcia Landy (2001).
5   Marcia Landy's chapter in *British Cinema, Past and Present* (2000) offers a different perspective – watching British cinema in America – but it remains a discussion framed around British national cinema.
6   Cf. Sue Harper (1994), Pam Cook (1996, 1997), Tony Williams (2000) and Landy (2001).
7   Mason and Mills appeared together in *Tiara Tahiti* (1962).
8   The BFI's 'Ultimate Film' project, which measured the top one hundred films based on UK cinema admissions, lists three Mason films in the top forty: No. 9 *The Wicked Lady* (18.4 million tickets sold), No. 10 *The Seventh Veil* (17.9 million) and No. 40 *Fanny by Gaslight* (11.7 million).
9   Although neither the city's nor the organisation's names are ever explicitly mentioned in the film.
10 Although according to Clive Hirschhorn and Sheridan Morley, *The Upturned Glass* (1947) was released just after *Odd Man Out*.
11 Cf. Geoffrey Nowell-Smith and Steven Ricci (1998), Andrew Higson and Richard Maltby (1999), Alastair Phillips and Ginette Vincendeau (2006), and Anthony Slide (2015).
12 Mason also insisted on a 'Portland clause' in his contract with Disney on *20,000 Leagues under the Sea* (1954), where the company was obligated to provide a weekly 16mm print of any Disney film for his daughter to watch (Mason 1981: 342).
13 Two of Portland Mason's obituaries (Anon. 2004a, 2004b) question these stories, but an interview with Morgan Mason supports them (Porter 1997).
14 See also Sue Harris (2015).
15 *Home James* is included as a DVD extra on the Odeon 'Best of British' release of *The Seventh Veil* (2009) and the Network release of *Odd Man Out* (2006). In 1967, Mason made a short film, *The London Nobody Knows*, which took a similar approach to viewing the city through an architectural, social and anthropological perspective.

3 POWER

1. Due to limited space, I am unable to explore Mason's television career here.
2. Despite Monaghan's official employment as a staff writer for the Masons, Mason notes he wrote very little (1981: 202).
3. Cf., for example, Robert Murphy (1997) and Higson and Maltby (eds.) (1999).
4. In 1936, Mason also made the independent production *Secret of Stamboul* and the Columbia Pictures-backed *Prison Breaker*.
5. Asquith had directed Mason in *Fanny by Gaslight* (1944).
6. Cf. Geoffrey Macnab (1993) and Murphy (1997).
7. Mason does not indicate whether this deal was an actor-only one or if it offered a producer or writer option.
8. The most famous example of this was Lew Wasserman's deal for James Stewart for *Winchester '73* (1950) where, in exchange for 50 per cent of the gross profits, the star took no salary (Mann 2008: 50).
9. Ironically, one of the reasons the relationship with Rose soured was the producer's attempt to align Mason to Universal, whom the star dismissed as 'splashing out' low-quality products (Mason 1981: 222).
10. In 1949, Mason starred (second billed) with Stanwyck in *East Side, West Side*.
11. Mason was approached to play the major role of Bolenger (with whom the eponymous heroine has an affair). However, he requested to play the novel's author (and film's narrator), Gustave Flaubert.
12. Bennett became Portland Mason's godmother, and it was an incident between Hedda Hopper and Bennett that resulted in the Masons later shifting their loyalty to Louella Parsons (Mason 1981: 401).
13. All taken from the Joseph Mankiewicz file, Margaret Herrick Library, Beverly Hills, California. One memo from Robert Lantz to Mankiewicz (dated September 10, 1957) says, 'It seems to be that Mason alone today is not a strong enough star to sell a major series …'

14 Letter from Mason to Mankiewicz in 1967, Margaret Herrick Library.
15 Mason notes in his autobiography that he signed with other agencies during this period.
16 Mason notes that it was championed on release by *Cahiers du Cinéma*, and Will Scheibel (2014) offers a detailed analysis of the film's reception.
17 *Cry Terror!* (1958) relies on Mason's believability as an ordinary American family man in the story of a family held hostage by terrorists.
18 The film was later made – without Harrington's involvement – as *The Pyx* (1973).
19 He also made the non-exploitation productions *Torpedo Bay* (1963 Italy/France) and *Los pianos mecánicos/The Uninhibited* (1965 Spain).
20 The third edition of Bondanella's seminal Italian film history (renamed from *Italian Cinema: from Neorealism to the present* to *A History of Italian Cinema*) includes a chapter on the *poliziotteschi*.
21 Cf. Bondanella (2009) and also Christopher Barry (2004) and Austin Fisher (2014).

4 PERFORMANCE

1 *Salem's Lot* was originally a two-part adaptation for American television but was re-edited for cinematic release.
2 Cf. James Naremore (1988), Peter William Evans (2001) and Amy Lawrence (2010).
3 'Mason appears to have as much contempt for *Salem's Lot* as I do', Tom Chick and Chris Hornbostel (2013).
4 Mason and Gielgud appeared on screen together five times: *Julius Caesar* (1953), *Frankenstein: The True Story* (1973), *11 Harrowhouse* (1974), *Murder by Decree* (1979) and *The Shooting Party* (1985).
5 *Duffy* (1968), *The Last of Sheila* (1973) and *Cross of Iron* (1977).
6 This is tied to racial identity, where the predominantly black audience aligns with the voice and power of Belafonte's character, overwhelming

the 'white' voice of Fleury (Mason) (even though it is discovered that the latter has black ancestry).

7 Although the play is entitled *The Seagull*, the film's title is *The Sea Gull*.
8 Susan M. White describes Mason's character in *Caught* with a different emphasis – 'the average Joe (who also happens to be James Mason)' (1995: 242).
9 Mason and Steiger appeared together in *Cry Terror!* (1958).

BIBLIOGRAPHY

Anon. (1946) 'Mr Mason talks about Mr Rank, and the "Quaint Folk" of films', *Daily Express*, December 16 (BFI Library).
Anon. (1947) Twentieth Century-Fox biography: 'James Mason' (Margaret Herrick Library).
Anon. (1954a) 'Feature Review: *A Star is Born*', *Motion Picture Herald*, October 2 (Warner Brothers archive, University of Southern California).
Anon. (1954b) '*A Star is Born* Review', *Film Bulletin*, October 18 (Warner Brothers archive, University of Southern California).
Anon. (1956) Warner Brothers contract file: *A Star Is Born* (Warner Brothers archive, University of Southern California).
Anon. (1967a) 'The Masonic touch', *Observer*, November 12 (BFI Library).
Anon. (1967b) 'Questions and Answers: James Mason on the Set of *Stranger in the House* (BFI Library).
Anon. (1968) 'A rejuvenated James Mason', *The Times*, June 6 (BFI Library).
Anon. (1975) ITC biography: 'James Mason – the Quiet Man of the 1970s' (BFI Library).
Anon. (1984) 'James Mason', *The Scotsman*, June 28 (BFI Library).
Anon. (2004a) 'Portland Mason', *Daily Telegraph*, June 3.
Anon. (2004b) 'Portland Mason', *Independent*, June 1.
Ashby, Justine and Andrew Higson (eds.) *British Cinema, Past and Present*, London & New York: Routledge.
Bacher, Lutz (1996) *Max Ophüls in the Hollywood Studios*, New Brunswick, NJ: Rutgers University Press.

Barry, Christopher (2004) 'Violent Justice: Italian Crime/Cop Films of the 1970s', in Ernest Mathijs and Xavier Mendik (eds.), *Alternative Europe: Eurotrash and Exploitation Cinema Since 1945*, London & New York: Wallflower Press: 77–89.

Behlmer, Rudy (ed.) (1993) *Memo from Darryl F. Zanuck: The Golden Years at Twentieth Century-Fox*, New York: Grove Press.

Bick, Ilsa J. (1994) '"That Hurts!": Humor and Sadomasochism in *Lolita*', *Journal of Film and Video*, Vol. 46, No. 2, Psychoanalysis and Film: 3–18.

Biskind, Peter (1974) 'Rebel without a Cause: Nicholas Ray in the Fifties', *Film Quarterly*, Vol. 28, No. 1: 32–38.

Bondanella, Peter (2009) *A History of Italian Cinema*, London & New York: Continuum.

Bonner, Hilary (1983) 'Third time lucky for rebel Mason?', *Mail on Sunday*, February 2 (BFI Library).

Bray Lower, Cheryl and R. Barton Palmer (2001) *Joseph L. Mankiewicz: Critical Essays with an Annotated Bibliography & Filmography*, Jefferson, NC, & London: McFarland.

Canby, Vincent (1973) 'James Mason', *Eugene Register-Guard*, August 19: 19.

Carman, Emily and Philip Drake (2015) 'Doing the Deal: Talent Contracts in Hollywood', in Paul McDonald, Emily Carman, Eric Hoyt and Philip Drake (eds.), *Hollywood and the Law*, London: BFI: 209–34.

Carman, Emily (2016) *Independent Stardom: Freelance Women in the Hollywood Studio System*, Austin: University of Texas Press.

Conway, Harold (1950) 'James Mason: I marked time as an actor', *Evening Standard* (BFI Library).

Cook, Pam (1996) *Fashioning the Nation: Costume and Identity in British Cinema*, London: BFI.

Cook Pam (ed.) (1997) *Gainsborough Pictures*, London & Washington: Cassell.

Crossley, Laura (2014) 'Indicting Americana: How Max Ophüls Exposed the American Dream in *Caught* (1949) and *The Reckless Moment* (1949)', *Studies in European Cinema*, Vol. 11, No. 2: 116–25.

Cunningham, Frank R. (2001) *Sidney Lumet: Film and Literary Vision*, Lexington: University of Kentucky Press.

Drazin, Charles (2007) *The Finest Years: British Cinema of the 1940s*, London & New York: I. B. Taurus.

Dyer, Richard (1998) *Stars*, London: BFI.

Edwards, Sydney (1970) 'Mason: third career', *Evening Standard*, May 16 (BFI Library).

Eleftheriotis, Dimitris (2001) *Popular Cinemas of Europe: Studies of Texts, Contexts and Frameworks*, London & New York: Continuum.

Emmett Long, Robert (ed.) (2001) *George Cukor: Interviews*, Jackson: University of Mississippi Press.

Erens, Patricia (1994) 'A Childhood at the Cinema: Latency Fantasies, the Family Romance, and Juvenile Spectatorship', *Wide Angle*, Vol. 16, No. 4: 24–56.

Evans, Peter and James Thomas (1958) 'And <u>now</u> James Mason plumps for <u>real</u> films', *Daily Express*, September 13 (BFI Library).

Evans, Peter William (2001) 'James Mason: The Man Between', in Bruce Babington (ed.), *British Stars and Stardom*, Manchester: Manchester University Press: 108–19.

——— (2005) *Carol Reed*, Manchester: Manchester University Press.

Finler, Joel W. (2003) *The Hollywood Story*, London & New York: Wallflower Press.

Fisher, Austin (2011) *Radical Frontiers in the Spaghetti Western: Politics, Violence and Popular Italian Cinema*, London & New York: I. B. Taurus.

Franklin, Olga (1953) 'James Mason: odd man out!', *Daily Sketch* (BFI Library).

——— (undated) 'The rudest man in America', *Daily Sketch* (BFI Library).

French, Philip (1984) 'A fine actor', *Observer*, June 19: 19 (BFI Library).

Frost, Jennifer (2011) *Hedda Hopper's Hollywood: Celebrity Gossip and American Conservatism*, New York: New York University Press.

Garvey, Adrian (2015) '"Steely Velvet": The Voice of James Mason', *Journal of British Cinema and Television*, Vol. 12, No. 2: 83–100.

——— (2016) 'Masculinity and Ageing in the Films of James Mason', in Lucy Bolton and Julia Lobalzo Wright (eds.), *Lasting Screen Stars: Images that*

Fade and Personas that Endure, Basingstoke, Hants.: Palgrave Macmillan: 141–55.

Gelley, Ora (2008) 'Ingrid Bergman's Star Persona and the Alien Space of Stromboli', *Screen*, Vol. 47, No. 2: 26–51.

Geraghty, Christine (2000) 'Re-examining Stardom: Questions of Texts, Bodies and Performance', in Christine Gledhill and Linda Williams (eds.), *Reinventing Film Studies*, London: Arnold: 89–110.

Gilbey Ryan (2003) 'The star of the sidelines', *Independent*, November 7 (BFI Library).

Glancy, Mark (2011) '*Picturegoer*: The Fan Magazine and Popular Film Culture in Britain during the Second World War', *Historical Journal of Film, Radio and Television*, Vol. 31, No. 4: 453–78.

Gordon, Bernard (1999) *Hollywood Exile, or How I Learned to Love the Blacklist*, Austin: University of Texas Press.

Gourlay, Logan (1952) 'Yes, it pays to be James Mason', *Sunday Express*, November 28 (BFI Library).

Hall, Gladys (undated) 'James Mason Notes' (Gladys Hall papers, Margaret Herrick Library).

Hall, John (1969) 'Mason in character', *Guardian*, May 10 (BFI Library).

Harper, Sue (1994) *Picturing the Past: The Rise and Fall of the British Costume Film*, London: BFI.

Harper, Sue and Justin Smith (2012) *British Film Culture in the 1970s*, Edinburgh: Edinburgh University Press.

Harris, Sue (2015) '*Toujours Delon*: The Script of Aging', in Nick Rees-Roberts and Darren Waldron (eds.), *Alain Delon: Style, Stardom, and Masculinity*, London & New York: Bloomsbury.

Hart, Henry (1954) 'Movie Review: *A Star is Born*', *National Board of Review* (Warner Brothers archive, University of Southern California).

Hellicar, Michael (1984) 'The odd man out who became a legend', *Daily Star*, July 28: 20 (BFI Library).

Hibben, Nina (1969) 'Making a film that is good enough for Huddersfield', *Morning Star*, June 6 (BFI Library).

Higson, Andrew and Richard Maltby (eds.) (1999) *Film Europe and Film America: Cinema, Commerce and Cultural Exchange 1920–1939*, Exeter: Exeter University Press.

Hirschhorn, Clive (1969) 'The mistake James Mason so regrets', *Sunday Express*, June 22 (BFI Library).

——— (1977) *The Films of James Mason*, Secaucus, NJ: Citadel Press.

Hirshberg, Jack (1948) Untitled press release, April 15 (Margaret Herrick Library).

——— (1949) Untitled press release, February 9 (Margaret Herrick Library).

Holmlund, Chris (2010) 'Celebrity, Aging and Jackie Chan: Middle-Aged Asian in Transnational Action', *Celebrity Studies Journal*, Vol. 1, No. 1: 96–112.

Houseman, John (1988) *Unfinished Business: A Memoir*, London: Columbus Books.

Hunter, Martin (2001) *Romancing the Bard: Stratford at Fifty*, Toronto & Oxford: Dundurn Press.

Irvin, Sam (2010) *Kay Thompson: From Funny Face to Eloise*, New York & London: Simon & Schuster.

Jones, Graham (1984) 'Odd man out – the one role James Mason never quite lost', *Daily Telegraph*, July 28: 13 (BFI Library).

Kemper, Tom (2010) *Hidden Talents: The Emergence of Hollywood Agents*, Berkeley: University of California Press.

Landy, Marcia (2000) 'The Other Side of Paradise: British Cinema from an American Perspective', in Justine Ashby and Andrew Higson (eds.), *British Cinema, Past and Present*, London & New York: Routledge: 63–79.

——— (2001) *British Genres: Cinema & Society, 1930–1960*, Princeton, NJ: Princeton University Press.

Lambert, Gavin (1958) 'Good-bye to Some of All That, *Film Quarterly*, Vol. 12, No. 1: 25–29.

Lawrence, Amy (1999) 'Trapped in a Tomb of Their Own Making: Max Ophüls's *The Reckless Moment* and Douglas Sirk's *There's Always Tomorrow*', *Film Criticism*, Vol. 23, No. 2: 150–66.

―――― (2010) 'James Mason: A Star Born Bigger than Life', in R. Barton Palmer (ed.), *Larger Than Life: Movie Stars of the 1950s*, New Brunswick, NJ, & London: Rutgers University Press: 86–106.

Lester, Joan (1950) 'What's gone wrong with James Mason?', *Reynold's News*, April 23: 3 (BFI Library).

Lewin, David (1983) 'The nearly man', *Mail on Sunday*, May 15: 67–69 (BFI Library).

Lowry, Suzanne (1981) 'Men for all seasons', *Sunday Express*, April 6 (BFI Library).

Macauley, Sean (2003) 'A master of melancholy', *The Times*, November 11 (BFI Library).

Macnab, Geoffrey (1993) *J. Arthur Rank and the British Film Industry*, Oxford & New York: Routledge.

―――― (2000) *Searching for Stars: Rethinking British Cinema*, London & New York: Cassell.

―――― (2003) 'Odd Man Out', *Guardian*, October 10 (BFI Library).

Man O'The People (undated) 'Really Mr Mason, I couldn't care less!', unknown newspaper (BFI Library).

Mann, Denise (2008) *Hollywood Independents: The Postwar Talent Takeover*, Minneapolis & London: University of Minnesota Press.

Mann, Roderick (1961) 'I'm just pig-headed, says James Mason', *Sunday Express*, January 1 (BFI Library).

―――― (1964) 'At 55, Mr Mason faces up to life without Pam and the cats', *Sunday Express*, April 26 (BFI Library).

―――― (1967) 'At 59, James Mason is a very mellow fellow', *Sunday Express*, August 18 (BFI Library).

―――― (1983) 'How Mr Mason lost that sinister image', *Sunday Express*, March 6 (BFI Library).

Marshall, P. David (2010) 'The Promotion and Presentation of the Self: Celebrity as Marker of Presentational Media', *Celebrity Studies Journal*, Vol. 1, No. 2: 35–48.

Mason, James (1945) 'Glamour', *Summer Pie*, London: Odhams Press: page unknown.

—— (1946a) 'I hate producers!', *Lilliput*, April: 305.

—— (1946b) 'Why I am going to America', *Winter Pie*, London: Odhams Press: 21.

—— (1946c) Letter to Hedda Hopper, December 29 (Hedda Hopper file, Margaret Herrick Library).

—— (1947) Title unknown, *Daily Mail*, January 24 (BFI Library).

—— (1948) 'Why I am afraid of going to Hollywood', *Cosmopolitan*, February: 147–48.

—— (1950) 'James Mason hits back at his critics', unknown publication (BFI Library).

—— (1973) Letter to Daniel Mann, March 16 (Daniel Mann papers, Margaret Herrick Library).

—— (1981) *Before I Forget*, Reading: Sphere Books.

—— (undated) 'Yes, I beat my wife', *Lilliput* (BFI Library).

—— (undated) 'Filming in Hollywood', *The Star*: 6 (BFI Library).

Mason, Pamela (1946) Letter to Hedda Hopper, December 20 (Hedda Hopper papers, Margaret Herrick Library).

McDonald, Paul (2013) *Hollywood Stardom*, Chichester, W. Sussex: Wiley-Blackwell.

McGilligan, Patrick (2011) *Nicholas Ray: The Glorious Failure of an American Director*, New York: It Books/HarperCollins.

McNally, Karen (2012) 'Damaged Beauty: Montgomery Clift, Tragedy and the Redefinition of a Star Image', in Kate Egan and Sarah Thomas (eds.), *Cult Film Stardom: Offbeat Attractions and Processes of Cultification*, Basingstoke, Hants: Palgrave Macmillan: 181–96.

Medhurst, Andy (1986) 'Dirk Bogarde', in Charles Barr (ed.), *All Our Yesterdays: 90 Years of British Cinema*, London: BFI.

Monaghan, Jno. P (1947) 'James Mason's answer to his fans', *Sunday Graphic*, April 13: 5 (BFI Library).

Morin, Edgar (1960) *The Stars* (translated by Richard Howard), London: Grove Press/ John Calder.

Morley, Sheridan (1989) *James Mason: Odd Man Out*, London: Weidenfeld & Nicolson.

———— (2002) *John Gielgud*, New York: Simon & Schuster.

Morrison, James (1998) *Passport to Hollywood: Hollywood Films, European Directors*, Albany: SUNY Press.

Mosely, Leonard (1952) 'No flags from me for Mr. Mason', *Daily Express*, November 14 (BFI Library).

———— (1996) 'Under the Shadow of Hollywood', in Charles Barr (ed.), *All Our Yesterdays: 90 Years of British Cinema*, London: BFI: 47–71.

———— (1997) 'Gainsborough after Balcon', in Pam Cook (ed.), *Gainsborough Pictures*, London & Washington: Cassell: 137–155.

———— (2007) 'British Film Noir', in Andrew Spicer (ed.), *European Film Noir*, Manchester: Manchester University Press: 84–111.

Naremore, James (1988) *Acting in the Cinema*, Berkeley & London: University of California Press.

Neve, Brian (1992) *Film & Politics in America: A Social Tradition*, London & New York: Routledge.

Nowell-Smith, Geoffrey (1998) 'Introduction', in Geoffrey Nowell-Smith and Steven Ricci (eds.), *Hollywood and Europe: Economics, Culture, National Identity 1945–95*, London: BFI: 1–18.

Osborne, John (1947) 'James Mason', *Life*, June 6: 33–40.

Parmentier, Marie-Agnes (2011) 'When David Met Victoria: Forging a Strong Family Brand', *Family Business Review*, Vol. 24, No. 3: 217–32.

Pearson, Roberta E. (1999) 'A Star Performs: Mr March, Mr Mason and Mr Maine', in Alan Lovell and Peter Krämer (eds.), *Screen Acting*, London & New York: Routledge: 59–74.

Phillips, Alastair and Ginette Vincendeau (eds.) (2006) *Journeys of Desire: European Actors in Hollywood*, London: BFI.

Plain, Gill (2006) *John Mills and British Cinema: Masculinity, Identity and Nation*, Edinburgh: Edinburgh University Press.

Porter, Monica (1997) 'The bizarre Hollywood childhood of James Mason's son', *Daily Mail*, October 24: 9.

Richards, Jeffrey (1990) 'James Mason: superstar who was an odd man out', *Daily Telegraph*, November 8: 21 (BFI Library).

Rollyson, Carl (2012), *Hollywood Enigma: Dana Andrews*, Jackson: University of Mississippi Press.

Russell, William (1984) 'James Mason: star of magnetism and menace', *Glasgow Herald*, July 28: 8 (BFI Library).

Scheibel, Will (2014) 'Bigger Than Life: Melodrama, Masculinity, and the American Dream', in Steven Rybin and Will Scheibel (eds.), *Lonely Places, Dangerous Grounds: Nicholas Ray in American Cinema*, Albany: SUNY Press: 177–88.

Sheldon, Joanna and David Meilton (1984) 'Veteran British star of almost a hundred films, James Mason dead', *Evening Standard*, July 27: 1, 5.

Shepherd, S. Rossiter (1946) 'Swelled head of James Mason', *People*, December 29 (BFI Library).

Sinyard, Neil (1986) *Filming Literature: The Art of Screen Adaptation*, London & Sydney: Croom Helm.

Slide, Anthony (2015) *A Special Relationship: Britain Comes to Hollywood and Hollywood Comes to Britain*, Jackson: University of Mississippi Press.

Spicer, Andrew (2003) *Typical Men: The Representation of Masculinity in Popular British Cinema*, London & New York: I. B. Taurus.

——— (2006) *Sydney Box*, Manchester: Manchester University Press.

Stott, Catherine (1969) 'The rebirth of James Mason', *Guardian*, November 26 (BFI Library).

Swinnen, Aagje (2012) 'Introduction: *Benidorm Bastards*, or the Do's and Don'ts of Aging', in Aagje Swinnen and John A. Stotesbury (eds.), *Aging, Performance, and Stardom: Doing Age on the Stage of Consumerist Culture*, Zurich: Lit Verlag: 7–18.

Sykes, Constance (1946), Letter to Hedda Hopper, September 4 (Hedda Hopper papers, Margaret Herrick Library).

Taylor, Weston (1969) 'Home, James: Mr Mason goes back to the mill', *News of the World*, April 27 (BFI Library).

Thomas, Sarah (2012) *Peter Lorre – Face Maker: Constructing Stardom and Performance in Hollywood & Europe*, New York & Oxford: Berghahn.

Turner, Graeme (2010) 'Approaching Celebrity Studies', *Celebrity Studies*, Vol. 1, No. 1: 11–20.

Vaughn, Dai (1995) *BFI Film Classics: Odd Man Out*, London: BFI.

Vincendeau, Ginette (2000) *Stars and Stardom in French Cinema*, London & New York: Continuum.

Wagstaff, Christopher (1992) 'A Forkful of Westerns: Industry, Audiences and the Italian Western', in Richard Dyer and Ginette Vincendeau (eds.), *Popular European Cinema*, Oxford & New York: Routledge: 245–62.

——— (1998) 'Italian Genre Films in the World Market', in Geoffrey Nowell-Smith and Steven Ricci (eds.), *Hollywood and Europe: Economics, Culture, National Identity 1945–95*, London: BFI: 74–85.

Ward, Paul (2013) 'Did You See James Mason in Town Today? A Case Study in Transatlantic and Local Identities in British Stardom', *Journal of Transatlantic Studies*, Vol. 11, No. 4: 403–22.

Warner, Jack (1954) 'Telegram to James Mason', Warner Brothers contract file for *A Star Is Born* (Warner Brothers archive, University of Southern California).

Webster, Jack (1982) 'Even at 73, James Mason's image still makes him blush', *Glasgow Herald*, September 11 (BFI Library).

Weisser, Thomas (1992) *Spaghetti Westerns – the Good, the Bad and the Violent*, Jefferson, NC, & London: McFarland.

White, Susan M. (1995) *The Cinema of Max Ophüls: Magisterial Vision and the Figure of Woman*, New York: Columbia University Press.

Williams, Tony (2000) *Structures of Desire: British Cinema 1939–55*, Albany: SUNY Press.

Wilson, Cecil (1962) 'As Mr Mason Makes His Peace with Rank' (BFI Library).

Websites

BFI 'Ultimate Film' research project: 'The Complete Chart', 2004: http://old.bfi.org.uk/features/ultimatefilm/chart/index.php. Accessed February 8 2016.

BFI 'Most Wanted: The Hunt for Britain's Missing Films', 2010: http://old.bfi.org.uk/nationalarchive/news/mostwanted/this-man-is-dangerous.html. Accessed February 8 2016.

Chick, Tom and Chris Hornbostel (2013), 'Thirty Years of Horror: *Salem's Lot*'. *Quarter to Three* media blog, October 22: http://www.quartertothree.com/fp/2013/10/22/thirty-years-horror-salems-lot-1979/. Accessed February 29 2016.

Moviemail.com film catalogue: 'British Classics from Odeon Entertainment', 2014: http://www.moviemail.com/special-offers/1460/British-Classics-from-Odeon-Entertainment/. Accessed February 8 2016.

Sandford, Christopher (2009) 'James Mason: Odd Man Out', *Bright Lights Film Journal*, April 30: http://brightlightsfilm.com/james-mason-odd-man-out/#.VsmaddCaWW4. Accessed February 20 2016.

Wasson, Sam (2006) '*Bigger Than Life*: The Picture, the Production, the Press', *Sense of Cinema*, February: http://sensesofcinema.com/2006/nicholas-ray-two-classics-revisited/bigger_than_life/. Accessed February 15 2016.

FILMOGRAPHY

LATE EXTRA (Albert Parker, Fox Film UK, UK 1935)
TWICE BRANDED (Maclean Rogers, G. S. Enterprises, UK 1936)
TROUBLED WATERS (Albert Parker, Fox Film UK, UK 1936)
PRISON BREAKER (Adrian Brunel, Columbia Grand, UK 1936)
BLIND MAN'S BLUFF (Albert Parker, Fox Film UK, UK 1936)
THE SECRET OF STAMBOUL (Andrew Marton, Wainwright/GFD, UK 1936)
THE MILL ON THE FLOSS (Tim Whelan, National Provisional, UK 1936)
FIRE OVER ENGLAND (William K. Howard, Korda, UK 1937)
THE HIGH COMMAND (Thorold Dickinson, Fanfare, UK 1937)
CATCH AS CATCH CAN (Roy Kellino, Fox Film UK, UK 1937)
THE RETURN OF THE SCARLET PIMPERNEL (Hans Schwartz, London Films, UK 1937)
I MET A MURDERER (Roy Kellino, Grand National, UK 1939)
THIS MAN IS DANGEROUS (Lawrence Huntington, Rialto/Pathé, UK 1941)
HATTER'S CASTLE (Lance Comfort, Paramount British, UK 1942)
THE NIGHT HAS EYES (Leslie Arliss, Associated British/Pathé, UK 1942)
ALIBI (Brian Desmond Hurst, British Lion, UK 1942)
SECRET MISSION (Harold French, Excelsior, UK 1942)

THUNDER ROCK (Roy Boulting, MGM, UK 1942)
THE BELLS GO DOWN (Basil Dearden, Ealing, UK 1943)
THE MAN IN GREY (Leslie Arliss, Gainsborough, UK 1943)
THEY MET IN THE DARK (Karel Lamac, Excelsior, UK 1943)
CANDLELIGHT IN ALGERIA (George King, British Lion, UK 1943)
FANNY BY GASLIGHT (Anthony Asquith, Gainsborough, UK 1944)
HOTEL RESERVE (Victor Hanbury, Lance Comfort and Max Greene, RKO, UK 1944)
A PLACE OF ONE'S OWN (Bernard Knowles, Gainsborough, UK 1945)
THEY WERE SISTERS (Arthur Crabtree, Gainsborough, UK 1945)
THE WICKED LADY (Leslie Arliss, Gainsborough, UK 1945)
THE SEVENTH VEIL (Compton Bennett, Box/GFD, UK 1945)
ODD MAN OUT (Carol Reed, Two Cities, UK 1947)
THE UPTURNED GLASS (Lawrence Huntington, Box/GFD, UK 1947)
CAUGHT (Max Ophüls, Enterprise/MGM, USA 1949)
MADAME BOVARY (Vincente Minnelli, MGM, USA 1949)
THE RECKLESS MOMENT (Max Ophüls, Walter Wanger/Columbia, USA 1949)
EAST SIDE, WEST SIDE (Mervyn LeRoy, MGM, USA 1949)
ONE WAY STREET (Hugo Fregonese, Universal, USA 1950)
PANDORA AND THE FLYING DUTCHMAN (Albert Lewin, Romulus/MGM, UK 1951)
THE DESERT FOX (Henry Hathaway, Twentieth Century-Fox, UK 1951)
FIVE FINGERS (Joseph Mankiewicz, Twentieth Century-Fox, USA 1952)
LADY POSSESSED (Roy Kellino and William Spier, Portland, USA 1952)
THE PRISONER OF ZENDA (Richard Thorpe, MGM, USA 1952)
FACE TO FACE (John Brahm and Bretaigne Windust, RKO, USA 1952)
CHARADE (Roy Kellino, Portland, USA 1953)
THE MAN BETWEEN (Carol Reed, London Films, UK 1953)
THE STORY OF THREE LOVES (Gottfried Reinhardt and Vincente Minnelli, MGM, USA 1953)
THE DESERT RATS (Robert Wise, Twentieth Century-Fox, USA 1953)
JULIUS CAESAR (Joseph Mankiewicz, MGM, USA 1953)

BOTANY BAY (John Farrow, Paramount, USA 1953)
THE TELL-TALE HEART (Ted Parmelee, UPA/Columbia, USA 1953)
THE CHILD (James Mason, Portland, USA 1954)
PRINCE VALIANT (Henry Hathaway, Twentieth Century-Fox, USA 1954)
A STAR IS BORN (George Cukor, Warner Bros., USA 1954)
20,000 LEAGUES UNDER THE SEA (Richard Fleischer, Disney, USA 1954)
FOREVER DARLING (Alexander Hall, MGM, USA 1956)
BIGGER THAN LIFE (Nicholas Ray, Twentieth Century-Fox, USA 1956)
ISLAND IN THE SUN (Robert Rossen, Twentieth Century-Fox, USA 1957)
CRY TERROR! (Andrew L. Stone, Andrew L. Stone/MGM, USA 1958)
THE DECKS RAN RED (Andrew L. Stone, Andrew L. Stone/MGM, USA 1958)
NORTH BY NORTHWEST (Alfred Hitchcock, MGM, USA 1959)
JOURNEY TO THE CENTRE OF THE EARTH (Henry Levin, Twentieth Century-Fox, USA 1959)
A TOUCH OF LARCENY (Guy Hamilton, Paramount, UK 1959)
THE TRIALS OF OSCAR WILDE (Ken Hughes, Warwick, UK 1960)
THE MARRIAGE-GO-ROUND (Walter Lang, Twentieth Century-Fox, USA 1961)
ESCAPE FROM ZAHRAIN (Ronald Neame, Paramount, USA 1962)
LOLITA (Stanley Kubrick, MGM, UK/USA 1962)
HERO'S ISLAND (Leslie Stevens, Portland, USA 1962)
TIARA TAHITI (Ted Kotcheff, Rank, UK 1962)
TORPEDO BAY (Bruno Vailati and Charles Frend, British Lion, Italy/France 1964)
THE FALL OF THE ROMAN EMPIRE (Anthony Mann, Paramount, USA 1964)
THE PUMPKIN EATER (Jack Clayton, Columbia, UK 1964)
LORD JIM (Richard Brooks, Columbia, UK/USA 1965)
GENGHIS KHAN (Henry Levin, Columbia, UK/USA/West Germany/Yugoslavia 1965)

LOS PIANOS MECÁNICOS/THE UNINHIBITED (Juan Antonio Bardem, Francos Film, Spain 1965)
THE BLUE MAX (John Guillermin, Twentieth Century-Fox, UK 1966)
GEORGY GIRL (Silvio Narizzano, Columbia, UK 1966)
THE DEADLY AFFAIR (Sidney Lumet, Columbia, UK 1966)
STRANGER IN THE HOUSE (Pierre Rouve, Rank, UK 1967)
THE LONDON NOBODY KNOWS (Norman Cohen, British Lion, UK 1967)
DUFFY (Robert Parrish, Columbia, UK/USA 1968)
MAYERLING (Terence Young, Warner Bros., UK/France 1968)
THE SEA GULL (Sidney Lumet, Warner Bros., UK/USA/Greece 1968)
AGE OF CONSENT (Michael Powell, Columbia, Australia 1969)
SPRING AND PORT WINE (Peter Hammond, EMI, UK 1970)
THE YIN AND YANG OF MR GO (Burgess Meredith, Ross International, UK/Canada 1970)
COLD SWEAT (Terence Young, EMI, France/Italy 1970)
BAD MAN'S RIVER (Eugenio Martin, Scotia International, Italy 1971)
KILL! (Romain Gary, Salkind, Spain/Italy/West Germany/France 1971)
HOME JAMES (Patrick Boyle, Yorkshire Television, UK 1972)
CHILD'S PLAY (Sidney Lumet, Paramount, USA 1972)
THE LAST OF SHEILA (Herbert Ross, Warner Bros., USA 1973)
THE MACKINTOSH MAN (John Huston, Warner Bros., UK/USA 1973)
FRANKENSTEIN: THE TRUE STORY (Jack Smight, Universal, UK/USA 1973).
11 HARROWHOUSE (Aram Avakian, Twentieth Century-Fox, UK 1974)
THE MARSEILLE CONTRACT (Robert Parrish, Warner Bros., UK 1974)
GREAT EXPECTATIONS (Joseph Hardy, Transcontinental, UK/USA 1974)
MANDINGO (Richard Fleischer, Paramount, USA 1975)
INSIDE OUT (Peter Duffell, Warner Bros., UK 1975)
AUTOBIOGRAPHY OF A PRINCESS (James Ivory, Merchant/Ivory, UK 1975)

KIDNAP SYNDICATE/LA CITTÀ SCONVOLTA: CACCIA SPIETATA AI RAPITORI (Fernando Di Leo, Gastaldi Film Italy, Italy 1975)
THE FLOWER IN HIS MOUTH/GENTE DI RISPETTO (Luigi Zampa, Zampa Film, Italy 1975)
THE LEFT HAND OF THE LAW/LA POLIZIA INTERVIENE: ORDINE DI UCCIDERE! (Giuseppe Rosati, Rosati Film, Italy 1975)
FEAR IN THE CITY/PAURA IN CITTÀ (Giuseppe Rosati, Rosati Film, Italy 1976)
VOYAGE OF THE DAMNED (Stuart Rosenberg, Avco Embassy, UK 1976)
JESUS OF NAZARETH (Franco Zeffirelli, ITC/RAI, Italy/UK 1977)
CROSS OF IRON (Sam Peckinpah, Avco Embassy, UK/West Germany 1977)
HEAVEN CAN WAIT (Warren Beatty and Buck Henry, Paramount, USA 1978)
THE BOYS FROM BRAZIL (Franklin J. Schaffner, Twentieth Century-Fox, USA/UK 1978)
THE WATER BABIES (Lionel Jeffries, Ariadne Films, Poland/UK 1978)
THE PASSAGE (J. Lee Thompson, Hemdale, UK 1979)
BLOODLINE (Terence Young, Paramount, USA/West Germany 1979)
MURDER BY DECREE (Bob Clark, EMI, UK/Canada 1979)
SALEM'S LOT (Tobe Hooper, Warner Bros., USA 1979)
NORTH SEA HIJACK (Andrew V. McLaglen, Universal, UK 1980)
IVANHOE (Douglas Camfield, Columbia, UK/USA 1982)
EVIL UNDER THE SUN (Guy Hamilton, Universal, UK 1982)
THE VERDICT (Sidney Lumet, Twentieth Century-Fox, USA 1982)
A DANGEROUS SUMMER (Quentin Masters, Filmco/McElroy & McElroy, Australia 1982)
YELLOWBEARD (Mel Damski, Hemdale, UK 1983)
THE ASSISI UNDERGROUND (Alexander Ramati, Cannon, USA 1985)
A.D. (Stuart Cooper, Vincenzo Labella, UK/Italy 1985)
THE SHOOTING PARTY (Alan Bridges, Edenflow/Reeve, UK 1985)
DR FISCHER OF GENEVA (Michael Lindsay-Hogg, BBC/Consolidated Productions, UK 1985)

INDEX

Note: n = endnote number

11 Harrowhouse 104–105, 123n
20,000 Leagues Under the Sea 65, 121n

A

A Place of One's Own 26, 128n
A Star Is Born 4, 24, 27, 44, 63, 65, 90–94, 95–96, 103, 112, 116–117
A Touch of Larceny 37, 74
Academy Awards 75, 90, 96
Adler, Buddy 70–71
Age of Consent 3, 36, 43, 51, 76, 107
Ageing 5, 8, 34–37
Aldrich, Robert 61
Alibi 26
Allen, Gracie 29
American Film Series 75
Andrews, Dana 60
Arliss, Leslie 15
Asquith, Anthony 44, 52, 122n
Audiences 9, 14, 17, 33, 34, 41

Autobiography of a Princess 77, 101–103

B

Bad Man's River 37, 76, 78, 79
Barefoot Contessa, The 67
Bathsheba 87
BBC2 13
Beatty, Warren 81
Beckham family 32
Bel Geddes, Barbara 61
Belafonte, Harry 96, 123n
Bells Go Down, The 26
Bennett, Constance 64
Bennett, Joan 64, 69
Bergman, Ingrid 10
Bickford, Charles 91–92
Bigger Than Life 4, 27, 31, 44, 51, 68–74, 95, 103, 112
Blind Man's Bluff 50
Blumenthal, A. Pam 61
Body and Soul 61
Bogarde, Dirk 17, 41
Bogart, Humphrey 67
Bond Street 37
Botany, Bay 65

Box, Betty 54
Box, Muriel 53
Box, Sydney 11, 45, 51, 53–55
Boys From Brazil, The 81
Branding 31–33
Brando, Marlon 35, 66, 88
Bridges, James 75
British cinema 2, 4–5, 13, 15–19, 26, 38, 51
British Lion 26, 65
British New Wave 38
Bronson, Charles 80, 98
Burns and Allen Show, The 29
Burns, George 29
Byronic 9, 10, 16, 39, 42

C

Cagney, James 58
Call for the Dead, A 114
Calvert, Phyllis 11
Cambridge University 3, 39
Campbell, Donald 87
Canby, Vincent 7
Candlelight in Algeria 26

INDEX 141

Cats in Our Lives, The 29
Caught 49, 59, 60–64
Celebrity 2, 3, 8, 27–33, 105, 120n
Charade 30, 51, 65
Charlie Feldman Agency (see Feldman, Charlie)
Chekov, Anton 105–107
Child, The 31, 51
Child's Play 7, 76, 77
Christie, Agatha 81
Cinemascope 70–72
Cinematograph Films Act of 1927 50
Class 16–18, 25, 38–42
Clift, Montgomery 35
Coburn, James 88
Coconut Grove 57
Cold Sweat 76, 79–80, 98–99
Colman, Ronald 25, 61
Columbia Pictures 54, 63, 96, 122n
Comedy 8, 38, 86, 103–108, 110, 119
Conte, Richard 80
Contracts 6–8, 13, 43–61, 64–66, 68, 74, 121n
Cooper, Gary 61
Cotton, Joseph 80
Cross of Iron 81, 123n
Cry Terror! 27, 74, 123n, 124n
Cukor, George 44, 91–94

D

Davis, Bette 58
Deadly Affair, The 76, 114–118
Dean, James 41
Decks Ran Red, The 80
Delon, Alain 41
Deluxe 71
Desert Fox, The 4, 27, 65
Desert Rats, The 65
Di Leo, Fernando 76, 80
Diana Productions 64
Dirty Harry 79
Disney, Walt 64, 65, 121n
Distribution networks 25–26, 43, 51, 53–55, 58–59, 61, 65–66, 70, 76
Donat, Robert 17
Duffy 78, 123n
Duvall, Shelley 1, 2

E

Ealing Studios 26
East Side, West Side 27, 59, 122n
Eastman 71
Einfeld, Charles 61–63
Elstree Studios 1
EMI 76
Enterprise Studios 59, 61–64
Eroticism 4, 16–17, 29, 37
European Emigres in Hollywood 24–25
Evil Under the Sun 81

Excelsior 26
Existentialism 20–25, 97, 99–101, 106, 119
Exploitation cinema 76–82
Expressionism 23, 72

F

Face to Face 65
Faith Healer 87
Fanny by Gaslight 11, 121n, 122n
Fear in the City 77, 79
Feldman, Charlie 68, 70
Figaro Inc. 66, 68
Film noir 25, 64, 66, 104
Fitzgerald, Geraldine 35
Five Fingers 65, 66–67, 68
Flower in His Mouth, The 76, 79, 100–101
Force of Evil 61
Forever Darling 27
Fox Film Corporation (see Twentieth Century-Fox)
Foxwell, Ivan 74
Friel, Brian 87

G

G.B. Morgan 26
Gainsborough Pictures 3, 11–17, 21, 24–25, 26, 48, 51–52, 76, 103, 112, 120n
Garfield, John 61
Garland, Judy 91–93

Gate Theatre, Dublin 87
Gaumont-British Film Corporation 51–53
Georgy Girl 4, 7, 38, 76, 78, 107
Gielgud, John 66, 86–90, 91, 94, 104, 123n
Goldwyn, Samuel 56, 60, 64
Gordon, Bernard 37
Gossip 5, 9, 18, 27–32, 47
Granada Television 13
Granger, Stewart 52
Grant, Cary 35–36, 74, 84
Great Expectations 76
Great St. Trinian's Train Robbery, The 31
Grodin, Charles 104–105
Guinness, Alec 87
Guthrie, Tyrone 86–87

H
Harrington, Curtis 81, 123n
Hathaway, Henry 44
Hatter's Castle 26
Havilland, Olivia de 58
Haywood, Susan 96
Heathcliff 10, 120n
Heaven Can Wait 4, 81
Hemmings, David 80, 85
Herbet Lom 13
Hero's Island 51, 74

Hitchcock, Alfred 22, 44, 74, 84–85
Home James 39–41, 96, 121n
Hooper, Tobe 84
Hopper, Hedda 28–29, 30, 53, 122n
Hotel Reserve 26
Houseman, John 75
Howard, Leslie 17
Howard, Trevor 104
HUAC 63
Huddersfield, Yorkshire 3, 31, 38–41
Hume, Cyril 71
Huntingdon Hartford 65
Huston, John 77

I
I Know Where I'm Going! 53
I Met a Murderer 26, 51–52
Island in the Sun 74, 95, 96
Italian cinema 76–82, 123n
Ivory, James 76, 101

J
Jaffrey, Madhur 101–103
James Mason: The Star They Loved to Hate 13
Johnson, Val 14
Jolie, Angelina 31
Journey to the Centre of the Earth 27

Joyce, James 37
Julius Caesar 4, 24, 44, 65–66, 87–90, 95, 123n

K
Kardashian family 32
Kaye, Clarissa (see Mason, Clarissa) 1, 3, 34, 37
Kellino, Pamela (see Mason, Pamela) 3, 18–19, 28–31, 34, 37, 50–53, 65, 77
Kellino, Roy 19, 50, 65
Kidnap Syndicate 77, 79–81
Kill! 36, 76, 79
King, Stephen 84
Korda, Alexander 50, 56
Kubrick, Stanley 1–2, 33, 37, 44, 107–111
Kubrick, Vivian 1, 2

L
Lady Possessed 51, 65
Lambert, Gavin 71
Lang, Fritz 64
Last of Sheila, The 36, 123n
Lastfogel, Abe 59, 62, 64
Late Extra 26, 50
Laughton, Charles 87
Le Carre, John 114
Left Hand of the Law, The 76, 79
Letter From an Unknown Woman 61

Lewin, Albert 59
Livesey, Roger 87
Lloyd, Danny 2
Lockwood, Margaret 11
Loew, David L. 61–63
Lolita 1, 2, 4, 7, 24, 33, 37, 44, 74, 107–111, 112
London Nobody Knows, The 96, 121n
Lost in the Stars 34, 75
Lumet, Sidney 7, 44, 76, 105–107, 114–118

M

Mackintosh Man, The 77, 78
Madame Bovary 59, 60, 63, 95
Maibaum, Richard 71
Man Between, The 24, 26, 65
Man in Grey, The 3, 11–14, 51, 84
Man in the Gray Flannel Suit, The 31
Mankiewicz, Joseph 44, 66–68, 87, 89, 122n, 123n
Mann, Daniel 34, 75
March, Fredric 90
Marlborough College 3, 39
Marriage-Go-Round, The 27, 37, 96, 107
Marseille Contract, The 77
Martin, Dean 31

Mason, Clarissa (see Kaye, Clarissa)
Mason, James
 appearance 2, 8, 10, 14, 21, 35–37, 81, 106
 cats 28–30, 33
 conscientious objector 18–19
 criticism of film industry 3, 14–15, 44–49, 52–53, 75–76, 78, 84
 contracts (see main entry Contracts)
 divorce 3, 29, 34, 77
 early years 3, 39, 41
 family 1–3, 28–31, 33, 51–53, 121n, 122n
 going to the USA 3, 4, 7, 9, 13, 23, 25, 27–28, 48, 56–57
 lawsuit 44, 55–56
 marriage 3, 18–19, 29–30, 37
 producer 45, 50–51, 55, 68–71
 rejection A194of roles 34, 53, 59, 65, 67–68, 75, 122n
 return to the UK 3–4, 7, 9, 23, 33, 37, 48, 74–75
 salary 6–7, 44, 49–50, 52–54, 59–60, 62, 65, 74–75, 77
 stage 3, 86–87, 120n
 voice 8, 10, 35, 83, 85–88, 95–103, 106, 112, 116

 work in Europe 3, 7, 15, 48, 75–81, 123n
 writer 6, 18, 26, 29, 33, 45–49, 113
 regional identity 5, 8, 34, 38–42, 83
 national identity 8, 15–20, 24–26, 33
Mason, Morgan 3, 30, 121n
Mason, Pamela (see Kellino, Pamela)
Mason, Portland 3, 30–31
McMillan, Kenneth 85
Measure for Measure 87
Melodrama 3, 11, 13, 16, 19, 23, 25, 73, 103, 112
Merchant, Ismail 76
Merenda, Luc 80–81
MGM 26, 48, 59, 61, 63, 65, 66
Mill on the Floss, The 26, 50
Mills, John 17–18, 41, 121n
Minnelli, Vincente 44
Monaghan, John 14, 28, 45, 122n
Murder by Decree 1, 2, 76, 81, 85, 123n

N

Nabokov, Vladimir 107
Naughton, Bill 39
New Hollywood 48, 58, 66
Newman, Paul 77

Newton, Robert   98
Nicholson, Jack   1, 2
Night Has Eyes, The   25, 120n
Niven, David   25
North by Northwest   4, 7, 22, 36, 44, 74, 84–85, 94, 112

O

Odd Man Out   4, 13, 20–25, 44, 95, 97–99, 103, 106, 119, 121n
Odeon Entertainment   26
Odets, Clifford   71
Oedipux Rex   87
O'Herlihy, Dan   119
Old Vic Theatre   86
Olivier, Laurence   81
Olsen, Christopher   70
One Way Street   59
O'Neil, Jennifer   100
Ophuls, Max   44, 49, 61–63, 64, 74, 112–113
Ostrer, Isidore   51
Ostrer, Maurice   53, 54

P

Palance, Jack   80
Pandora and the Flying Dutchman   26, 27, 59, 65
Paper Chase, The   75
Paramount decrees   49, 57
Paramount Pictures   26, 54–56, 65, 114
Parker, Al   50, 52, 54

Parsons, Louella   28, 47, 53, 122n
Pathe   26
Peck, Gregory   81
Peckinpah, Sam   81
Pinkett Smith, Jada   32
Pitt, Brad   31
Poe, Edgar Allen   96–97
Poliziotteschi filone   79–81, 98, 123n
Polonsky Abraham   61
Portland Pictures   30, 74
Powell, Michael   44, 76
Power, Tyrone   14
Prince Valiant   65
Prisoner of Zenda, The   65
Private Life of Don Juan, The   50
Production Code Administration   63, 71
Pumpkin Eater, The   38, 95, 100

Q

Quiet American, The   67–68

R

Rank Organisation   13, 19, 34, 44, 47, 51–55, 76
Rank, J. Arthur   15, 34, 44, 52, 53
Ray, Nicholas   44, 71–74

Rebel Without a Cause   71
Reckless Moment, The   4, 27, 44, 59, 63–64, 74, 112
Redgrave, Vanessa   105
Reed, Carol   20–22, 24, 44, 65, 97–98, 119
Reed, Oliver   80
Reinhardt, Wolfgang   63
Renoir, Jean   64
Rialto   26
RKO   26
Roberts Productions   61
Rochester, Edward   10, 120n
Romulus Films   59
Rose, David   54–56, 122n
Rossen, Robert   44
Roueche, Berton   70
Rush, Barbara   70
Ryan, Kathleen   21
Ryan, Robert   61

S

Salem's Lot   84–86
Sanders, George   50
Scarlet Street   64
Schell, Maximillian   115
Sea Gull, The   7, 76, 77, 105–107, 124n
Secret Beyond the Door   64
Secret Mission   26
Sadism   10–11, 13, 17, 19, 21, 24–26, 61, 83–84, 99, 112
Sellers, Peter   108
Selznick, David   50

Selznick, Myron   50
Seventh Veil, The   4, 11, 13, 14, 21, 44, 53–55, 60, 84, 103, 121n
Sexuality   16–17, 37
Shepperton Studios   26
Shining, The   1–3, 119
Shooting Party, The   4, 44, 81, 95, 100, 123n
Signoret, Simone   105
Silva, Henry   80
Skouras, Spyros   54
Smith, Jaden   32
Smith, Will   32
Smith, Willow   32
Sorry, Wrong Number   60
Spaghetti Westerns   77, 79
Spring and Port Wine   39, 75, 77, 114
Spy Who Came in from the Cold, The   114
Stanwyck, Barbara   60, 122n
Star families   31–32
Steiger, Rod   114, 124n
Stewart, James   60, 122n
Stone, Andrew L.   74
Story of Three Loves, The   65

Stratford Shakespeare Festival, Ontario   87
Switzerland   3, 23, 77

T

Talent agencies   6, 28, 50, 55–56, 58–59, 68, 70, 82
Talking Pictures   13
Tell-Tale Heart, The   96
Ten Feet Tall' (article)   70
The Association of Cine Technicians   15, 52
The British Film Producers Association   15, 52
They Met in the Dark   26
Third Man, The   74
This Man is Dangerous   26
Thunder Rock   26, 95
Tiara Tahiti   37, 121n
Todd, Ann   13
Troubled Waters   50, 51
Twentieth Century-Fox   26, 29, 45, 50–1, 54, 60, 64–70

U

United Artists   61, 65
United Productions of America   96
Universal Pictures   55, 59, 122n

Upturned Glass, The   25, 51, 53–54, 95, 121n

V

Verdict, The   7, 44, 76, 81

W

Wanger, Walter   59, 63–64
Warner Bros.   56, 57, 61
Warner, David   105
Warner, Jack   57
Water Babies, The   39
Wicked Lady, The   11, 15, 52, 121n
Widescreen   70–71
William Morris Agency   58, 59, 68
Winters, Shelley   108
Woman in the Window, The   64
World War II   18–19, 25, 78, 99

Y

Yin and Yang of Mr Go, The   37
Yorkshire Television   39, 96

Z

Zanuck, Darryl   45, 64–66, 68, 70, 74, 120n